Sandra Bullock

Other books in the People in the News series:

Maya Angelou
Tyra Banks
David Beckham
Beyoncé
Fidel Castro
Kelly Clarkson
Hillary Clinton
Miley Cyrus
Ellen Degeneres
Leonardo DiCaprio
Hilary Duff
Zac Efron
Brett Favre
50 Cent
Al Gore
Tony Hawk
Salma Hayek
LeBron James
Jay-Z
Derek Jeter
Steve Jobs
Dwayne Johnson
Angelina Jolie
Jonas Brothers
Kim Jong II
Coretta Scott King
Ashton Kutcher

Spike Lee
Tobey Maguire
Eli Manning
John McCain
Barack Obama
Michelle Obama
Danica Patrick
Nancy Pelosi
Tyler Perry
Queen Latifah
Daniel Radcliffe
Condoleezza Rice
Rihanna
Alex Rodriguez
Derrick Rose
J.K. Rowling
Shakira
Tupac Shakur
Will Smith
Gwen Stefani
Ben Stiller
Hilary Swank
Justin Timberlake
Usher
Denzel Washington
Serena Williams
Oprah Winfrey

Sandra Bullock

By Sandy Gade Algra

LUCENT BOOKS
A part of Gale, Cengage Learning

GALE
CENGAGE Learning

Detroit • New York • San Francisco • New Haven, Conn • Waterville, Maine • London

LIBRARY OF CONGRESS CATALOGING-IN-PUBLICATION DATA

Algra, Sandy Gade.
  Sandra Bullock / by Sandy Gade Algra.
    p. cm. -- (People in the news)
  Includes bibliographical references and index.
  ISBN 978-1-4205-0428-6 (hardcover)
1. Bullock, Sandra--Juvenile literature. 2. Motion picture actors and
actresses--United States--Biography--Juvenile literature. I. Title.
  PN2287.B737A45 2011
  791.4302'8092--dc22
  [B]
                                                                    2010046753

Lucent Books
27500 Drake Rd
Farmington Hills MI 48331

ISBN-13: 978-1-4205-0428-6
ISBN-10: 1-4205-0428-2

Printed in the United States of America
1 2 3 4 5 6 7 15 14 13 12 11

Printed by Bang Printing, Brainerd, MN, 1st Ptg., 03/2011

Contents

Fame and celebrity are alluring. People are drawn to those who walk in fame's spotlight, whether they are known for great accomplishments or for notorious deeds. The lives of the famous pique public interest and attract attention, perhaps because their experiences seem in some ways so different from, yet in other ways so similar to, our own.

Newspapers, magazines, and television regularly capitalize on this fascination with celebrity by running profiles of famous people. For example, television programs such as *Entertainment Tonight* devote all their programming to stories about entertainment and entertainers. Magazines such as *People* fill their pages with stories of the private lives of famous people. Even newspapers, newsmagazines, and television news frequently delve into the lives of well-known personalities. Despite the number of articles and programs, few provide more than a superficial glimpse at their subjects.

Lucent's People in the News series offers young readers a deeper look into the lives of today's newsmakers, the influences that have shaped them, and the impact they have had in their fields of endeavor and on other people's lives. The subjects of the series hail from many disciplines and walks of life. They include authors, musicians, athletes, political leaders, entertainers, entrepreneurs, and others who have made a mark on modern life and who, in many cases, will continue to do so for years to come.

These biographies are more than factual chronicles. Each book emphasizes the contributions, accomplishments, or deeds that have brought fame or notoriety to the individual and shows how that person has influenced modern life. Authors portray their subjects in a realistic, unsentimental light. For example, Bill Gates – the cofounder and chief executive officer of the software giant Microsoft – has been instrumental in making personal computers the most vital tool of the modern age. Few dispute his business savvy, his perseverance, or his technical expertise, yet critics say he is ruthless in his dealings with competitors and driven more by his desire to maintain Microsoft's dominance in the computer industry than by an interest in furthering technology.

In these books, young readers will encounter inspiring stories about real people who achieved success despite enormous obstacles. Oprah Winfrey – the most powerful, most watched, and wealthiest woman on television today – spent the first six years of her life in the care of her grandparents while her unwed mother sought work and a better life elsewhere. Her adolescence was colored by pregnancy at age fourteen, rape, and sexual abuse.

Each author documents and supports his or her work with an array of primary and secondary source quotations taken from diaries, letters, speeches, and interviews. All quotes are footnoted to show readers exactly how and where biographers derive their information and provide guidance for further research. The quotations enliven the text by giving readers eyewitness views of the life and accomplishments of each person covered in the People in the News series.

In addition, each book in the series includes photographs, annotated bibliographies, timelines, and comprehensive indexes. For both the casual reader and the student researcher, the People in the News series offers insight into the lives of today's newsmakers – people who shape the way we live, work, and play in the modern age.

America's Sweetheart

Although America's sweetheart is a slight misnomer for half-German actress Sandra Bullock, it is a title she earned early in her Hollywood career. Perhaps the title fits because, in a business crowded with young, surgically enhanced blondes trying to be the next "It girl," Bullock seems happy just to be herself. With brown hair, brown eyes, a slightly misshapen nose from a childhood accident, and a scar above one eye, she is not the stereotypical silver screen beauty. In fact, when she was cast in her breakout role as Annie Porter in the hit action-thriller *Speed* she said, "I knew the studio wanted a busty blonde with long legs, but the director, Jan de Bont, fought for me."[1] Like Annie, an ordinary girl who finds herself in extraordinary circumstances, Bullock won over the audience because she was so believable. Yet there was something else about her that captivated audiences. After that film, guys didn't just want to watch Bullock, they wanted to date her; girls didn't just admire Bullock, they wanted to be friends with her.

Bullock is a major movie star, ranked by *Forbes* magazine in 2010 as the highest-paid actress in Hollywood. But she has built a career on coming across as a regular person. As Bill Bennett, the director of her 1996 film *Two If by Sea*, explains, "The thing that is so endearing about Sandy is that she is normal."[2] While other actresses might cringe at such a description, Bullock has been catapulted to stardom because of it. Her popularity with moviegoers has never depended on being seen at clubs or parties

Not the typical Hollywood beauty, Sandra Bullock launched to stardom because of her ability to relate to audiences as an ordinary girl.

on the arm of the hottest men in Hollywood. Instead, in role after role, Bullock has chosen characters that audiences can relate to, cry with, cheer for, and laugh at.

Jill of All Genres

Bullock's résumé includes leading roles in a wide range of film genres: dramas, thrillers, sci-fi, action films, and her mainstay, comedies. Bullock's breakout roles were in the action films *Demolition Man* (1993) and *Speed* (1994). Even though acting

*The legal drama **A Time to Kill**, starring Matthew McConaughey (left) and Sandra Bullock, allowed Bullock to show more than just her comedic talent.*

took a backseat to action in those movies, Bullock created characters that were more than women in danger. Amid the nail-biting action and special effects, she exhibited a talent for comic relief that audiences appreciated.

Comedies have been the hallmark of Bullock's career. She is best known for her roles in a subgenre of comedy, romantic comedies. Some of her most popular are *Miss Congeniality* (2000), *Two Weeks Notice* (2002), and *The Proposal* (2009). These films also allowed Bullock to shine in another subgenre of comedy, physical comedy, in which the humor comes from the way the actors use their bodies. As her friend and director Anne Fletcher says, "There aren't that many women in this industry who will take the challenge of doing physical comedy."[3] Whether Bullock was falling down in a tight dress and heels in *Miss Congeniality* or running naked into her costar in *The Proposal*, she committed to the scene. In turn, audiences turned out in theaters, making these two of the most successful comedies of her entire career.

Bullock's dramatic films have not been as consistently successful as her comedies. Her first dramatic role after becoming a household name in 1994 was in *A Time to Kill* (1996), costarring Matthew McConaughey. The film, which was based on a John Grisham book of the same name, dealt with issues of race and injustice in the case of an African American man on trial for the murder of two white men. Bullock played Ellen Roark, a legal student helping the defense lawyer (McConaughey) win the case. The legal drama gave Bullock a chance to show she had more than comedic talents; the film grossed over $100 million and proved to critics that Bullock could handle a serious role.

Unfortunately for Bullock, a wartime drama she undertook the same year did not go over as well. Bullock costarred with Chris O'Donnell in *In Love and War* (1996), based on the true story of the young novelist Ernest Hemingway and his nurse. Critics gave the film lukewarm reviews and noted a lack of chemistry between the two actors. Bullock's performance was also panned. For example, *San Francisco Chronicle* reviewer Barbara Schulgasser criticized Bullock's choice to play her character as "snippy rather than warm."[4] Indeed, aside from a few notable exceptions such as *Crash* (2005) and *The Blind Side* (2009), Bullock's dramatic films have not appealed to critics or to audiences the way her comedies have.

Nevertheless, in more than twenty years of making movies, Bullock has continued to vary her roles, weathering the pressure of success or the failure of a film as it comes. She has managed not only to keep her longtime, loyal fans but also to reach new audiences with each new role that she takes.

America's Got Her Back

No matter the genre, Bullock's fan base is devoted to her regardless of how well her films perform. However, in 2010 when news broke that her husband, Jesse James, had cheated on her with three different women, Bullock received an outpouring of support from Americans who had never particularly followed her career. Online comments about stories regarding her husband's infidelity and their resulting divorce bore messages of support and admiration for Bullock. One woman summed up the feelings of many when she wrote, "We love Sandra Bullock and wish her every happiness as she moves on with her life."[5]

Moving forward with the support of her fans, the future is whatever Bullock chooses to make of it. Despite the major changes in her personal life—such as the secret adoption of her son, Louis, and the pursuit of her soy candle company and other side businesses—Bullock has emphatically denied she is giving up on making movies. Whenever she does return to the big screen, her fans are sure to be ready for her.

Chapter 1

International Beginnings

Sandra Annette Bullock was born in Arlington, Virginia, on July 26, 1964, but her story begins much earlier and a continent away. Sandra's father, John, was a hard-working man with a varied history even before he met Sandra's mother, Helga. He hailed from a large family of eight children and went from being a blacksmith in Alabama to a music student at Juilliard, one of the world's most prestigious performing arts schools, in New York City. John was a talented singer, but his career path changed when he took a civilian job with the Pentagon (the headquarters for the U.S. Department of Defense) in Nuremburg, Germany.

It was there that he met Helga Meyer, his beautiful secretary and an aspiring opera singer. Opera was Helga's true passion. It was John's too. As Sandra tells it, "It's one of those great stories: she would bicycle her way to work and he'd drive the Mercedes by her. And she was the fledgling opera singer, and he didn't know it, and she didn't know he was into opera."[6] John was recently divorced when he met Helga, and quite a bit older, so he took his time in beginning a new romance. The two eventually married in Germany.

John's work for the government took the couple back to the northern Virginia suburbs of Washington, D.C., where their first daughter, Sandra, was born in 1964. As a family, they made Arlington, Virginia, their official home base, but they traveled often to Europe, mostly Germany and Austria, while Helga performed opera and John taught voice classes. It was just the kind of traveling artistic lifestyle that many people dream of.

Opera

Opera, which literally means *work* in Italian, is much more than just a musical. It is a performing art that requires very talented singers, musicians, and scenery and costume designers. Together these artists tell a dramatic story whose words are sung instead of spoken. Opera began in Italy in the 1500s, spread throughout Europe, and is now performed around the world. Many operas are performed in theaters called opera houses, but operas can also be seen on television and at movie theaters and heard on the radio. There are operas in almost every language in the world. One of the most famous German operas is by Wolfgang Amadeus Mozart. It is called *Die Zauberflöte*, or *The Magic Flute*.

Sprechen Sie Deutsch? (Do You Speak German?)

As a young child, Sandra lived in both the United States and Europe, and was exposed to two very different cultures. Her international lifestyle required her to speak two languages and make friends on two continents. As a result, she didn't grow up as the all-American girl. Under her mother's German influence, she wore German-style clothes rather than American brands. She also missed out on being a Brownie (a junior member of the Girl Scouts of America) like many American girls her age. However, with an American father and a part-time life in the United States, she did not have a typical German childhood either . Sandra adapted well to the challenge of growing up in two cultures. "When you're a kid and you do it that young in the way that we did it, you don't know any differently," she says. "So we knew that you'd get on a plane and you'd go to a different country and you meet new friends and you figure out a language and you learn that language, or you figure out the culture and you immerse yourself into that culture."[7]

For six years, Sandra enjoyed these experiences with her parents as an only child. Then, in March 1970, the Bullock family expanded with the birth of Sandra's sister, Gesine (pronounced ge-ZEE-na). For Sandra, having a baby around was a difficult adjustment. She recalls, "I was horrible to her! My grandmother swears I tried to kill her."[8] Even as they got older, Sandra would pick on Gesine: "I remember abusing her a bit, but I really didn't understand her, because she was just a demure, sweet, smart little girl who was well-behaved. And I, of course, was none of the above. I was the wild child."[9]

Growing up, Sandra Bullock (right) and her sister Gesine (left) juggled their time between American life in Virginia and German life in Nuremburg.

The two sisters and their parents continued to shuttle between homes in Virginia and Nuremburg. Sandra and Gesine spent hours at the theaters where their mother performed. The exposure to theater, music, and foreign languages had a significant impact on both girls. Sandra, who speaks fluent German, studied piano, gymnastics, and ballet. She even kept a poster of her favorite ballet dancer, Rudolf Nureyev, on her bedroom wall. Gesine says growing up in Europe was "like a fairy tale."[10] Sandra agrees; she remembers it as "all castles and cafes and not a single car."[11]

An Actress Is Born

Sandra first performed on stage when she was eight years old. She was a child extra in an opera production her mother was in. "In Europe when my mother performed I was always in the operas as some dirty Gypsy kid," says Sandra. "In every opera, you'll notice there's some dirty Gypsy child, and that was me."[12] Perhaps it was the applause, or the chocolate she received in praise of her work, but something about those early performances sparked her interest in acting as a career. In fact, an entry from her childhood diary testifies to Sandra's interest in acting at a young age. When she was around eight years old she wrote, "I want to be an actor because you get to sing, dance and meet people from different countries."[13]

When she was nine years old, Sandra unofficially began her film career using her father's video camera. The film, which was rediscovered by her mother in the mid-1990s, shows Sandra in full costume and big blonde wig playing the role of a secretary. Sandra was driven early on, not only to act but also to direct and produce. About the short film Sandra says, "I cast it, did the wardrobe, I got all my neighbors to partake in the production."[14]

A Life-Threatening Accident

The Bullocks' fairy-tale life nearly ended when Sandra was eleven years old. While back in the United States and working on some property he owned in the central Virginia countryside, Sandra's father John had a terrible accident. He slipped from a bulldozer he was using to clear the land. The out-of-control machine rolled over him, crushing his legs, breaking several vertebrae (bones) in his back, and almost severing his arm. Because he was working alone in a remote area, twenty-four hours passed before anyone discovered what had happened.

Sandra was the one who took the phone call from the hospital informing the family of the accident. She had to break the news to her mother: "All I remember is, my mom had to leave, and I was sitting on the curb with my sister [who was] screaming her head off."[15] Because young children are not always allowed to visit seriously injured patients, and because of ongoing health complications that kept him in the hospital, Sandra and her sister were unable to see him regularly for several months while he recuperated. Even though it was a difficult time for the young Sandra, it prepared her for her own tough times to come.

Wanting to Fit In

Around the time Sandra began junior high school, the family settled permanently in Virginia. The transition was difficult for her. "All I wanted to do was just be like the other girls in my school," she remembers. Her mother encouraged her to embrace her international identity, and failed to understand how important it was for Sandra to be like the other girls. "My mother was like, 'Be original,' with her German accent and all. I was like, 'Shut up, Helga!' All I wanted was a pair of Levi's straight-leg jeans, and all my mom had for me was green velvet bell-bottoms from Germany. Guess what? Bell-bottoms were out."[16]

Despite her mother's protests, Sandra was determined to look like everyone else. When she was fourteen, she got a job cleaning an insurance company office and used her earnings to buy "typical American" clothes she thought would help her fit in. As she put it, "I became incredibly ordinary. Everything I owned was monogrammed."[17]

Helga didn't conform to her daughter's expectations about what a mom should look like either. She dressed and acted differently than the other mothers in the neighborhood. Sandra remembers,

Sandra Bullock poses with her mother Helga and father John in 1998. Despite Helga's encouragement to embrace her international identity, Sandra longed to fit in with other American girls.

"It used to drive me crazy as a kid: I wanted her to be preppy, to be conservative, and she would have none of it. In my eyes, she was too sexy to be a mother."[18] Helga insisted on embracing her own style, even though it made Sandra self-conscious. "She did what she did and didn't care what people thought," says Sandra. "But as a kid, I was like, 'Oh, dear God, please make her stop and be normal.' I wanted an ordinary mom."[19]

Sandra's mother also set her own rules when it came to food. She kept her family on a strict macrobiotic diet, which means that they ate whole grains and organic vegetables that had not been treated with pesticides. Sandra remembers that her mother "made sure every morsel placed in front of [us] was pure and without anything artificial no matter what the cost."[20] Although a macrobiotic diet is more common today, in the 1960s and 1970s it was rare. Sandra admits, "It wasn't fun as a kid. We went to the neighbors for our Cheetos and the good stuff."[21] Even the festive parties that the Bullocks regularly hosted at their home featured healthy dishes and snacks.

Another thing that made Sandra self-conscious was her nose, which was broken accidentally by her sister. When Sandra was young, she got a little too close as Gesine opened the garage door. Gesine's elbow landed squarely on her sister's face. The result was a broken nose that Sandra now jokes about, saying, "People think it's a nose job, but seriously, why would I choose this one?"[22] This was not the only injury that gave her face its unique character. She also has a small scar above her left eye from falling and hitting her head on a rock. While these flaws and scars gave her the one-of-a-kind look she would someday be famous for, she viewed them at the time as just one more obstacle to fitting in at school.

Being Bullied

The more Sandra strove to fit in, the more fellow students teased and even bullied her. Bullock says the abuse was both emotional and physical, and has admitted that she was beat up by other students. Sandra was definitely not in the popular crowd yet—she had just one close friend, a boy named Tracy. Her mother didn't understand the social struggles her daughter faced at school. "I'd go to my mother and say, 'Today I had my head cracked into a locker,' but she wouldn't understand. 'Why would little kids do that to my daughter?' she'd ask. Mom didn't realize you didn't have to have a reason."[23]

Bullying had a lasting impact on the future actress. "I can still remember the first and last names of every one of those kids who were mean to me,"[24] she says. Being bullied taught Sandra the importance of being nice to everyone, no matter what. She vowed never to be like the bullies who taunted her. A desire to be nice to people was not the only trait that Sandra honed during these socially challenging years. As she puts it, "It's what made me have a sense of humor and thick skin."[25]

Sandra Bullock, seen here as a high school senior, claims that because of her strong desire to fit in during junior high and high school, she became extremely ordinary.

After joining the cheerleading squad in high school, Sandra Bullock (center) quickly went from outcast to part of the popular crowd.

Seeking acceptance from her peers, in high school Sandra put her interest in drama aside and traded artistic pursuits for typical American sports-related activities like cheerleading. Because she had previously trained in gymnastics, she was a natural, nailing tough moves like back handsprings and aerials (hands-free cartwheels) for the Generals at Washington-Lee High School.

After she joined the cheerleading squad, Sandra noticed that classmates who had never even spoken to her before suddenly wanted to be her friend. Seemingly overnight she had gone from outcast to all-American cheerleader. She had finally earned her spot in the popular crowd—but promptly realized it wasn't the right group for her after all. "Suddenly I woke up," she says. "I had turned into this cookie-cutter uniform."[26] She realized that being popular wasn't everything, and returned to activities that made her happy, like drama.

Bright Lights, Big City

Sandra graduated from high school in 1982. Her parents hoped she would go on to college at her father's alma mater, Juilliard. But Sandra did not feel she was prepared for that level of study or dedication. When a friend offered her a spare application for East Carolina University (ECU), in Greenville, North Carolina, Sandra

The Meisner Technique

The Meisner Technique is an acting technique developed by Sanford Meisner, who taught at the Neighborhood Playhouse in New York City. The Meisner Technique requires actors to thoughtfully consider why they are doing or saying something instead of just repeating what is written on the page. One important exercise for this technique is called repetition. In this exercise, two actors face each other

Sanford Meisner (far right) developed the Meisner Technique, which resulted in the actor portraying their role in a more believable manner.

and repeat an observation about each other. For example, one actor might say, "You're happy." The other would say "*I'm* happy," and the first would say, "You're *really* happy," and so on, and so forth. This allows the actors to be more spontaneous and react to what their partner is saying rather than just saying what they are told to say. The end result of employing the Meisner Technique is that the actor is more believable to the audience.

applied and was accepted. She remembers it took her only a week to make the decision to enroll there. At ECU Sandra was an active student. She majored in drama and balanced schoolwork, parties, and football games with roles in productions such as *Peter Pan*, *Stage Door*, and *The Three Sisters*. Ultimately, though, Sandra left college just a few credits shy of graduation to move to New York City and become a full-time actress.

When Bullock packed up her Honda Accord and drove to New York in 1986, she felt like somewhat of a pioneer. She says, "I went knowing one person, and I was kind of glad because you could start from scratch."[27] As she tried to break into the theater, she supported herself by bartending and waiting tables. Once she was mugged at gunpoint by a drug addict while leaving work, but refused to give up her hard-earned $186 in tips. "I just walked [away] and I kept thinking: 'Just don't shoot me in the spine,'" she says. "It was stupid but I think I knew enough about his mannerisms; he was just as scared as I was."[28] She was not shot and went back to the restaurant unharmed.

A Rocky Professional Start

Like all hopeful young actors, Bullock faced numerous rejections, which she tried not to let get her down. "There's so much rejection," she says. "If you take it to heart, you're lost."[29] She reinforced her efforts to audition for and get good parts by dedicating herself to the study of the Meisner Technique at a well-known acting school called the Neighborhood Playhouse in New York City. That sort of persistence helped her remain positive while she practiced her skills in just about any acting job that came her way. She jokes that for some jobs, "You'd have to go out to New Jersey and bring your own clothes and make-up and act horribly."[30]

Bullock finally got a break when an acting job in the off-Broadway play *No Time Flat* earned her a positive review in the *New York Times*. Though on the whole the production was not well received, reviewers singled out Bullock for praise. "The other performances are ... dim, with the possible exception of

Bullock (right) gained her most visible role to date in 1990 with the part of Tess McGill in a television show based on the popular movie Working Girl. The show was canceled after eight episodes.

Sandra Bullock as the daughter," wrote *New York Times* reviewer Mel Gussow. "She, at least, has a spark of forthrightness and a Southern manner."[31] This positive review, along with another by renowned theater critic John Simon, helped Bullock secure her first agent.

Over the next four years, Bullock started to make an impression in show business. In particular, she caught the eye of the producers of a new television comedy series based on the movie *Working Girl*. Bullock was up for the part of Tess McGill, a role originated by Melanie Griffith in the 1988 film. After eight grueling auditions, she won the part and made Los Angeles her new home base. The show aired on NBC in 1990 but, unlike the film, was not a huge success. It was canceled after only eight episodes. Even though it was her most visible role to date, Bullock remembers it as "the worst experience I've ever had in my life. I knew it was going to fail and I was hoping [it would]."[32] She was already prepared to pursue roles on stage and in movies if the television series did not succeed. In fact, big-screen film projects were exactly what were in store for her.

Chapter 2

Speeding
to Success

At the age of twenty-six, Bullock was on the cusp of becoming a steadily employed actress. Over the next several years, her career was jump-started with a role in the high-profile action movie *Demolition Man*, which eventually led to her role in *Speed*, the film whose success made her a household name. Despite this, as her career progressed through the 1990s, Bullock learned that not all her movies were bound to be box office successes.

Delayed Opening

In 1990, Bullock had one failed television series behind her and was eager to pursue roles in movies rather than television. Based on her work in the series *Working Girl*, Bullock was offered a role in executive producer Roger Corman's film *Fire on the Amazon*. Corman was known in Hollywood as the "King of 'B' Movies." That is, his movies did not have large budgets and were not widely released in movie theaters. Most were released directly to video. Bullock had really only had roles in minor projects thus far, so she happily accepted the part. However, while filming on location in the Amazon, Bullock dealt with a bad case of nerves as she filmed her first love scene. The production faced its own problems. Three years after it was made, the film had a limited release; that is, it was only screened in a few theaters.

Bullock's next big project, *Love Potion No. 9* (1992), was a new milestone for her. It was her first costarring role in a movie made by a major studio, Twentieth Century Fox. She played Diane Barrow, a geeky psychobiologist whose shy colleague shares a magic love potion with her. In a case of life imitating art, Bullock found love on the set with her leading man, actor Tate Donovan. Bullock was absolutely smitten with Donovan. At the time she gushed about him "There's nobody that means more to me, and I know for a fact that I mean the most to him, in that certain way. I can't explain why things worked out the way they did."[33]

Like *Fire on the Amazon* before it, this movie's release was also delayed. When it finally opened in theaters in November 1992, it did not make much money. The film was not well received by critics either. Eugene Levy of *Variety* said that *Love Potion No. 9* was characterized by "lack of real wit and comic vitality, [and an] absence of star names."[34] For Bullock, it would be at least another year before the list of star names included hers.

Demolishing the Competition

After *Love Potion No. 9*, Bullock won parts in several films that gave her name a little boost in Hollywood. For example, she earned a small role in *The Vanishing* (1993) costarring Jeff Bridges and Keifer Sutherland, and then a part in *The Thing Called Love* (1993), about a group of young songwriters trying to break into the Nashville country music scene. In the film, Bullock sings a song she cowrote called "Heaven Knocking on My Door." The song was supposed to depict a failed attempt at songwriting, and Bullock recalls, "I took great pleasure in making it as bad as possible."[35] These two films and another small role in *Wrestling Ernest Hemingway* (1993) opposite renowned actor Robert Duvall helped Bullock's film career gain momentum.

Ironically, it was a role that she did not actually audition for that changed Bullock's career dramatically. One night, while painting her stark white bathroom walls a sunny yellow, she received a call offering her a role in producer Joel Silver's *Demolition Man*, starring Sylvester Stallone and Wesley Snipes. It was unusual for

Sandra Bullock's performance alongside Sylvester Stallone (middle) and Benjamin Bratt (right) in Demolition Man *caught the attention of movie reviewers and film directors.*

a relatively unknown actress to get a job without an audition, but the timing was in her favor. Actress Lori Petty had left the project only three days before filming began, and the part of Lenina Huxley had to be recast as soon as possible to keep the filming schedule on track. A production executive had been quick to suggest Bullock. In a blur, she arrived on set, met her famous costars, and never finished painting her bathroom.

With major action stars attached and an equally big budget, *Demolition Man* was a significant opportunity for Bullock, whose previous movies had small casts and even smaller budgets. As she puts it, "I was used to small little talkie films, where all you have is the other person."[36] Landing a role in a star-studded, big-budget action movie was a huge change. Sharing the screen with two box office stars like Stallone and Snipes would increase her visibility in Hollywood and with audiences. Whereas *Love Potion No. 9* grossed less than $1 million at the box office, *Demolition Man* grossed more than $14 million in just its first weekend in theaters.

Bullock's high-energy performance caught the attention of movie reviewers such as Hal Hinson of the *Washington Post*. In his review, Hinson specifically mentioned Bullock's role in the film as "a spunky, restless cop named Huxley."[37] Film directors also took note of Bullock's performance. One in particular, Jan de Bont, was so impressed that even though several actresses including Bullock auditioned, he all but insisted she be the one cast in an action-thriller he was making about a bomb-rigged bus, called *Speed*.

The Girl from the Bus Movie

Bullock's intention after *Demolition Man* was to take a break from action movies, but as she searched for her next project, an action script caught her eye. It was unlike anything she had read before. It was about a psychopath who plants a bomb on a Los Angeles bus. The bomb is rigged to explode if the speed of the bus drops below 50 miles (80km) per hour. Bullock was keen to

The role of Annie Porter, opposite Keanu Reeves (left), in the action movie Speed *helped launch Sandra Bullock's A-list career.*

play the pivotal role of Annie Porter, a passenger who ends up driving the bus for most of the film. She remembers her audition, which included sitting in a chair pretending to drive a bus by holding a pretend steering wheel while delivering her lines: "I felt ridiculous. ... But you have to commit and just let go for those 15 minutes."[38] Her costar Keanu Reeves felt the same as Bullock regarding the awkward audition experience, saying, "It was two actors in a room pretending to drive a bus and falling on the ground."[39]

After the audition, studio executives were not convinced that Bullock was right for the part. De Bont insisted she play Porter, however, saying, "She had such an incredible freshness."[40] Meanwhile, Bullock was being cautioned about pursuing the part at all. Bullock's business associates and even her personal acquaintances dismissed the film, thinking its unusual plot about a wayward bus ride was a recipe for failure. In the end, De Bont got his way and Bullock accepted the role opposite Reeves. Bullock is quick to show her appreciation for the director who helped to launch her career. Bullock says, "[De Bont] fought for me, and I appreciate that more than he'll ever know."[41]

Jan de Bont

Speed director Jan de Bont was born in the Netherlands on October 22, 1943. He studied at the Amsterdam Film Academy and initially worked as a cinematographer. Sometimes called a director of photography, a cinematographer is responsible for filming the images that appear onscreen. After working as a cinematographer on several American action films such as *Die Hard* and *Lethal Weapon 3*, De Bont was hired to direct *Speed*. Because of its success, De Bont went on to direct *Twister* (1996) and the sequel to his first hit, *Speed 2: Cruise Control* (1997). His most recent work as a director was on *Lara Croft Tomb Raider: The Cradle of Life* (2003).

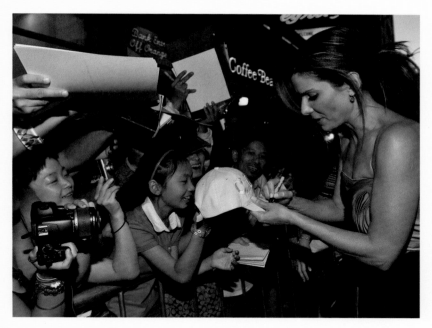

At the Los Angeles premiere of **All About Steve** *Sandra Bullock talks with fans and signs autographs. Bullock has humbly adapted to her growing fame and high-profile status.*

Speed was released on June 10, 1994. It was an instant hit. The movie grossed almost $15 million in its opening weekend and more than $100 million at the box office overall. This was far beyond the movie's stars' expectations. When asked if she expected *Speed* to do as well as it did, Bullock said, "Not in a million years. Because all people did was make fun of us. We were The Bus Movie."[42]

Bullock's Fame Grows

It wasn't just that the movie was a hit; Bullock was too. Reviewers and audiences were drawn to Bullock's gutsy style and believable performance. Movie reviewers, who only knew Bullock from her role in *Demolition Man*, were impressed. For example, a review in *Rolling Stone* magazine reported Bullock stole the movie with her performance. James Berardinelli, of Reelviews .net, said that Bullock "[possessed] enough charisma and spunk not to get outshone by her co-stars."[43] Bullock modestly attributes the film's success to its unique nature, explaining that "we were a little more human and real on film than people in action films used to be."[44]

Bullock was so easy to relate to that fans began approaching her to tell her she reminded them of someone they knew, or that her performance in *Speed* made them really believe she was an ordinary person who found herself in an extraordinary situation. She was increasingly accosted by fans and autograph seekers while out to dinner and even had to start using a pseudonym, a fake name, when she checked into hotels so as to maintain her privacy. These were unusual and unexpected experiences for Bullock; she did not yet see herself as a movie star. Before one appearance on *The Late Show with David Letterman*, for example, Bullock did not even realize that the huge crowds waiting outside the studio were there to see her. When her friends confirmed all those people were there to see her, she was overwhelmed. Over time, though, she adapted to her high-profile status. Said Jon Turteltaub, the director of *While You Were Sleeping* (1995), "She's handling it like she handles everything—humbly and happily."[45]

Switching Genres

After back-to-back successes in *Speed* and *Demolition Man*, it might have seemed natural that Bullock follow up with another action movie. Although she would revisit that genre in her career, her next film was a complete departure from the high-speed action that made her famous. Bullock's next significant role was as the lead in the 1995 romantic comedy hit *While You Were Sleeping*. Bullock was immediately interested in the role of Lucy Moderatz, a subway token collector who thinks she is in love with a stranger in a coma, but actually ends up falling in love with his wide-awake brother. The script, which explored the trials of love, appealed to Bullock because she happened to be enduring the

The Rom Com Genre

Unlike a traditional comedy, a romantic comedy—popularly known as rom com—revolves around a love story. Sometimes the couples are already together, but often these films are about two people falling in love amid a series of funny events and obstacles that keep them apart until the happy ending. William Shakespeare's plays *Much Ado About Nothing* and *A Midsummer Night's Dream* are considered to be the basis for modern-day rom coms because they are love stories about the funny ways two people become a couple. Several of Bullock's films fit in this genre, including *While You Where Sleeping, Forces of Nature, Two Weeks Notice,* and *The Proposal.*

pain of a real life breakup with Tate Donovan at the same time. Bullock says, "The script came to me at a time when I could relate to the sadness of the character. I identified with a girl for which nothing seems to go like it's supposed to."[46] Although the role was supposed to be played by Demi Moore, Bullock won the part not just because of her talent but because Moore's schedule and salary demands prevented her from taking the role.

Though Bullock had become famous for doing action movies, *While You Were Sleeping* allowed her to showcase her talent for romantic comedy. In the film, there are no action sequences, no bus chases, and no explosions. Instead, Bullock's portrayal of Lucy relies on sensitivity and humor, especially when her character is mistaken as the fiancée of the man in the coma by his family. This plot twist is further complicated when Lucy falls in love with the brother of her supposed fiancé. Of the film and Bullock's performance, renowned film critic Roger Ebert said, "Light romantic comedy is one of the trickiest of all movie genres. Usually, it doesn't work. …But [this film] works."[47] Audiences agreed; *While You Were Sleeping* was the number one movie in the United States in its opening weekend.

Sandra Bullock earned her first Golden Globe nomination in 1996 for While You Were Sleeping. *Her first Golden Globe win came in 2010, pictured, for her role in* The Blind Side.

Award-Winning Actress

With critical adulation came awards nominations. In 1995, her role in *Speed* earned her nominations for four MTV Movie Awards and she took home three: Best Female Performance, Most Desirable Female, and Best On-Screen Duo with her costar Keanu Reeves. The next year, Bullock earned three more MTV Movie Awards nominations for her roles as Angela Bennett in the 1995 cyber-thriller *The Net* and as Lucy in *While You Were Sleeping* (though she did not take home any awards). Also in 1996 she was nominated for a Golden Globe for Best Performance by an Actress in a Motion Picture–Comedy or Musical for her work in *While You Were Sleeping*. Though she did not take home the award (Nicole Kidman did for her performance in *To Die For*), it was an impressive achievement considering it had been only three years since her first major movie was released. Soon, though, Bullock would learn that early critical acclaim was no guarantee that her next films would be hits.

Box Office Bombs

After making four movies in two years, Bullock ramped up her schedule and worked almost non-stop. Within eighteen months, four Bullock films were released: *Two If by Sea*, *A Time to Kill*, *In Love and War*, and *Speed 2: Cruise Control*. Unlike her first big films, though, several of these movies struggled to find favor with audiences.

The first movie she made after *Speed* and *While You Were Sleeping* was another romantic comedy costarring comedian Denis Leary called *Two If by Sea*. Bullock played Roz, the girlfriend of a petty thief (played by Leary) who aims to settle down after completing a final robbery. The filmed opened in January 1996 at number ten, and after only three weeks had all but disappeared from theaters. Still, Bullock found a way to appreciate the film's disastrous failure: After two blockbusters, the pressure to do better with each successive film was off. As she put it, "The best thing that happened was that I completely stank and it was horrible."[48] She had officially survived her first failure, an important learning experience for her.

Bullock had several more chances to learn this lesson. One of the most significant failures of her career came in 1997 with her participation in the sequel *Speed 2: Cruise Control*. In the film, costarring Jason Patric as her boyfriend, Bullock reprised her role as Annie Porter. Although the film was set on a cruise ship, the plot was similar to the original: A disgruntled employee of the cruise liner hijacks its computer system and takes control of the ship, planning to crash it and steal diamonds that are stored on board. Even though her original costar, Keanu Reeves, declined to return as Jack Traven, Bullock was encouraged by film executives and her own staff to play Porter. Looking back, she acknowledges it was not her best professional decision. "My biggest regrets after *Speed* are things that people talked me into because they were 'a sure hit' and I didn't want to do them and I did them and they were bombs," she says. "*Speed 2* was one of the biggest [bombs]."[49]

The film was panned by almost all major reviewers, whose harsh criticism got right to the point. *Washington Post* critic Desson Howe called the film "the worst movie of the summer,"[50] while reviewer Stephen Hunter labeled it a "titanic dud."[51] Critics were just as harsh about Bullock's performance and one went so far as to suggest that her time as a leading lady was short-lived. Despite such glum predictions, the coming years in Bullock's career would be some of her most successful and cement her position in Hollywood history.

Chapter 3

Making Movies, Making History

After the failure of *Speed 2: Cruise Control* in 1997, Bullock tried to take greater control over her career choices. She did this in part by taking roles she personally wanted to play, rather than roles her business associates advised her to take. Between 1998 and 2000, Bullock starred in five hit movies: *Hope Floats* (1998), *Practical Magic* (1998), *Forces of Nature* (1999), *28 Days* (2000), and *Miss Congeniality* (2000). Her career was further boosted by some noteworthy achievements that set her apart from her peers in Hollywood. Indeed, during this period Bullock proved she was more than the average actress by making Hollywood history with her accolades, awards, and box office successes.

The Walk of Fame

In 2002, Bullock starred in three more hit films. These showed her range as an actress: a psychological thriller called *Murder by Numbers*, the feel-good drama *Divine Secrets of the Ya-Ya Sisterhood*, and the romantic comedy *Two Weeks Notice*. These helped earn Bullock a star on the Walk of Fame. Formally known as the Hollywood Walk of Fame, it is eighteen blocks of sidewalks studded with stars emblazoned with the names of notable figures in the entertainment industry. It is an honor for an actor to receive a star, and altogether only about 2,500 people are recognized there.

Sandra Bullock was honored with a star on the Hollywood Walk of Fame in 2005.

On March 24, 2005, Bullock received her own star. About accepting this tribute, Bullock jokes, "I no longer feel compelled, because of this honor, to carve my name into every wet cement board on a sidewalk."[52] Of note was the fact that before Bullock accepted this honor, she requested that her star be located next to the star honoring Keanu Reeves, her friend and costar from *Speed*. This was the first time a request of this kind had been made. Quipped Bullock about her unusual request, "I needed someone to watch my back, and he said he'd do it."[53] The organizers relented and both Bullock and Reeves' stars are located at 6801 Hollywood Boulevard in Los Angeles, California. Appropriately, Bullock received her star on the day of the release of what was to be another of her most successful films, *Miss Congeniality 2: Armed and Dangerous* (2005).

A Winning Proposal

Bullock next took roles in movies that were much smaller successes. In 2006, she teamed up with Reeves in the fantasy-drama *The Lake House* and also played real-life author Harper Lee in the historical drama *Infamous*. These dramatic films did not attract audiences the way Bullock's comedies did. Disappointed viewers presumed that Bullock and Reeves would share a lot of time onscreen, as they had been paired in *Speed*, but *The Lake House* showed the actors in separate scenes for the majority of the film. *Infamous* struggled in part because it covered the same subject as the award-winning film *Capote*, which had been released just the year before.

In 2009, however, Bullock returned to the romantic comedy genre that she was known for. In *The Proposal*, costarring her good friend Ryan Reynolds, Bullock played Margaret Tate, an overbearing boss who forces her assistant, played by Reynolds, to marry her so she can obtain a visa to legally remain in the United States. The film earned Bullock her biggest opening weekend ever, with a number one spot and over $30 million in ticket sales. Fans had been waiting seven years since Bullock's last appearance in a rom com, and audiences were glad to see her back in form. Reviewer Geoff Berkshire of *Metromix Chicago* put it plainly, saying, "Romantic comedy fans will get what they want."[54] The film delivered the humor and romance that was expected, and audiences opened their wallets and filled theaters as a result.

The Proposal, *a romantic comedy co-starring Ryan Reynolds, earned Sandra Bullock her biggest box-office opening weekend.*

A Winning Ensemble

On May 6, 2005, the film *Crash* was released in theaters. Bullock played the role of Jean Cabot (opposite onscreen husband played by Brendan Fraser), but she was by no means the lead actor. The film tells the interconnected story of several characters in Los Angeles, and is therefore best described as an ensemble piece; that is, a film with no lead stars, but rather multiple supporting actors. The film deals with somber issues such as racism and urban violence. It was a critical success and even won three Academy Awards, including Best Motion Picture of the Year. Though Bullock personally did not win any acting awards for her role, the entire cast was awarded with the Broadcast Film Critics Association's Critics' Choice Award for Best Acting Ensemble.

New Standard of Success

Bullock had an even bigger impact in 2009 in *The Blind Side*. Based on the book by Michael Lewis, *The Blind Side* tells the true story of a wealthy Tennessee family who adopted a homeless African American teenager who became a college graduate and a professional football player. Bullock played Leigh Anne Tuohy, the mother who takes in the young man.

Interestingly, Bullock's role in *The Blind Side* was one she almost did not take. She waited almost a year before meeting Tuohy in person, and it took a lot of convincing from director John Lee Hancock before Bullock felt she could handle the role of a devoutly Christian woman who adopts a child off the street. Bullock had not often played a mother onscreen and she did not feel that she would be able to do the important story or the character's religious and maternal values justice. Bullock admits, "I . . . don't think I could have done this role even five years ago, but . . . having a family of my own helped clarify the dynamics

In 2009, Sandra Bullock brought the true story of football player Michael Oher's childhood to the big screen. In the film The Blind Side, *Bullock played Oher's adoptive mother Leigh Anne Tuohy.*

in my head."[55] At the director's nearly nonstop urging, Bullock relented and the role, which had previously been turned down by Julia Roberts, was hers.

When *The Blind Side* was released on November 20, 2009, it opened at number two, with box office sales of $34 million. Typically, a movie does its best business in its opening week, and then ticket sales fall. But an unusual thing happened: In the second week, ticket sales for *The Blind Side* increased by almost 20 percent. In the third week, the movie rose to number one, beating out the popular *Twilight: New Moon* vampire saga. Interestingly, the story resonated with a variety of markets. Its themes of family love and succeeding against the odds attracted women and families to the theater. The movie's focus on professional football also appealed to men who sought a great sports story. As *San Francisco Chronicle* reviewer Mick LaSalle pointed out, "Bullock is most of the fun here . . . [but] college football aficionados may find more to enjoy here—inside jokes, riffs on the rivalries between various teams and cameo appearances by famous coaches."[56] As the 2009–2010 holiday season wore on,

Best and Worst Actress

Every year since 1981, a group of cinema fans and show business journalists has poked fun at the Hollywood awards hype by "honoring" the year's *worst* movies and performances. Called the Golden Raspberry Award Foundation, the group holds a ceremony in Los Angeles on the day before the Academy Awards. There the "winners" are announced and awarded the not-so-coveted Golden Raspberry trophy, or Razzie, a golfball-sized raspberry attached to an empty film reel and spray-painted gold, worth $4.79.

Sandra Bullock cheerfully accepts her Razzie, a spray-painted gold raspberry trophy that "honors" the year's worst performances, for her role in the box-office bomb **All About Steve.**

To her chagrin, in 2010 Golden Globe and Academy Award–winner Bullock was also a two-time Razzie winner for her performance in the box-office bomb *All About Steve*. The movie was panned by critics, audiences, and the Razzie nominating committee alike. Reviewers called the film dreadful, awful, and idiotic. Bullock was a good sport about it all. She showed up in person at the March 6 Razzies ceremony and cheerfully collected awards for Worst Actress and Worst Screen Couple (shared with costar Bradley Cooper). She even took the stage to accept her Worst Actress trophy pulling a red wagon full of *All About Steve* DVDs—a gift, she quipped, to all the Razzie voters. One day later, Bullock took home the Oscar, becoming the first actor to win a Best Actress Academy Award and a Worst Actress Razzie in a single year.

The Blind Side continued to perform well at the box office, so much so that after only seven weeks in theaters, it had grossed over $200 million.

While several movies have achieved this level of sales, *The Blind Side*'s success was historic: *The Blind Side* was the first movie with only one female lead to take in more than $200 million. At the age of forty-five, Bullock had set an enviable new standard in Hollywood. When the news broke, Warner Brothers. executive Dan Fellman boasted, "I think *Blind Side* has another $30 million left."[57] In fact, *The Blind Side* grossed more than $255 million in theaters, solidifying Bullock's place in Hollywood history.

Golden Girl

The Proposal and *The Blind Side* did not just garner attention for Bullock because the movies were popular; critics were also impressed by her acting. About her part in *The Proposal*, Peter Travers of *Rolling Stone* magazine said that Bullock's "genuine comic skills appear to be ageless."[58] *Los Angeles Times* critic Betsy Sharkey likewise raved about her performance in *The Blind Side*, saying, "Bullock blows in like a tornado. ... She nails the character."[59] *USA Today* reviewer Claudia Puig went so far as to say, "This is Bullock's movie, and it is perhaps her best role [to date]."[60]

The Hollywood Foreign Press Association, the organization that presents the annual Golden Globe Awards, was likewise impressed by Bullock's performances. In December 2009, its members nominated Bullock for two awards: Best Performance by an Actress in a Motion Picture–Comedy or Musical for *The Proposal* and Best Performance by an Actress in a Motion Picture–Drama for *The Blind Side*. In response to the nominations, Bullock said, "I am beyond stunned. Just to be included in the company of these amazing women I have so admired through the years has left me slack-jawed with awe."[61] At the January 2010 awards ceremony, Meryl Streep won the comedy Golden Globe for her performance in *Julie & Julia*, but a delighted Bullock took home the drama Golden Globe for *The Blind Side*. More than a decade after her first nomination for her role in *While You Were Sleeping*,

Despite her self-doubt, Sandra Bullock took home an Academy Award for her performance in **The Blind Side.**

Bullock had become a Golden Globe winner. Said Bullock, "It's crazy that this is happening now, cause it usually happens at the beginning, and then if you can continue with your career, that's great. ... [To win now], it's great."[62]

Her Golden Globe was not the last major award Bullock won in 2010. Bullock was stunned when two weeks later she was nominated for an Academy Award for Best Actress in a Leading Role in *The Blind Side*. At one point, she proclaimed to a room full of reporters, "I'm *so* not winning an Oscar!"[63] Despite her self-doubt, news outlets and blogs favored her to win. All eyes were on Bullock on March 7, 2010, when she arrived with her husband, Jesse James, at the Academy Awards ceremony.

When Bullock was announced as the winner, the audience erupted with applause, though Bullock herself hardly seemed to react. Taking the stage, Bullock thanked all those involved with the film, and said, "I have so many people to thank for my good fortune in this lifetime...[to] everyone who showed me kindness when it wasn't fashionable, I thank you."[64]

Highest-Paid Actress in Hollywood

In light of her major awards and phenomenal box office success, Bullock's salary for her next starring role will likely reach $20 million. This is an impressive achievement for an actress who began her career working for free on student productions and earned an estimated $500,000 for her breakout role in *Speed*. Bullock has since increased her earnings per picture. In fact, in August 2010, Bullock was ranked by *Forbes* magazine as Hollywood's highest-paid actress based on earnings from films and other deals between June 2009 and June 2010. During that time period, Bullock earned $56 million. In comparison, Reese Witherspoon and Cameron Diaz tied for second place with earnings of $32 million, followed by Jennifer Aniston, who earned $27 million.

Although Bullock's success as an actress is undeniable, she does not limit herself to achieving success onscreen. In fact, Bullock has been successful in a number of endeavors that have nothing to do with being a Hollywood movie star.

Chapter 4

Offscreen Successes

Since the mid-1990s Bullock has cemented her superstar reputation and built a solid career as an actress. Less well known, however, is her work behind the camera and outside the movie business. As owner of Fortis Films, successful restaurants, and a line of soy candles and as a generous philanthropist, Bullock puts as much attention and hard work into her offscreen endeavors as she puts into her film roles.

Going Behind the Camera

Soon after her early success in feature films, Bullock decided she wanted to not only act in movies but influence which movies ultimately get made. This is typically the job of a production company, so Bullock started her own. She formed Fortis Films in 1996 with her sister, Gesine. (*Fortis* means strength and perseverance in Latin.) Gesine had just finished law school and was looking for a new direction. Bullock says she hired her sister because of "her tastes and our [complementary] similarities and differences."[65] Bullock appointed her father CEO (chief executive officer) and also brought on board her friend from her waitressing days in New York City, Maggie Biggar, as vice president of production. While the women had plenty of combined education and useful experience, they were newcomers to running a production company themselves. But according to Gesine, after a while they "realized that it's chaotic, no matter how much you know."[66]

Sisterly Support

In 2005, Bullock's sister, Gesine Bullock-Prado, resigned from her role as president of Fortis Films. She later moved to Montpelier, Vermont, to start her own business, a bakery called Gesine Confectionary. Crowds flocked to the store opening, not just for the cookies and croissants, but also to catch a glimpse of Sandra Bullock, who came to show her support for Gesine's new venture with her husband, Ray. The business expanded to include a mail order service in 2009. The same year, Gesine also published her first book, *Confections of a Closet Master Baker: One Woman's Sweet Journey from Unhappy Hollywood Executive to Contented Country Baker.* (In paperback, the book is called *My Life from Scratch: A Sweet Journey of Starting Over, One Cake at a Time.*) The book was written as a tribute to Helga Bullock, who Gesine and Sandra insist threw the best parties.

Bullock, who thus far had made her career in front of the camera, found producing to be a rewarding experience. As she puts it, "It makes me feel like a proud parent. You'll be there at two in the morning, behind the monitor with greasy hair, and then the actors will do something that just inspires you."[67] She was hesitant to relinquish her role as an actress completely, however. Therefore, in 1998, Bullock opted to take on the challenge of both starring in and producing a feature-length movie, *Hope Floats.*

"Two Whole Jobs"

Hope Floats starred Bullock, Harry Connick Jr., and Gena Rowlands. The film was a quiet success and showed her colleagues how committed Bullock was to being both an actress and a producer. Said Martin Shafer, president of production company Castle Rock

The movie **Hope Floats** *was produced by Sandra Bullock. She also starred in the film with Harry Connick Jr.*

Entertainment, "I've never worked with a star who takes the producing chores as seriously as she does. She really does two whole jobs."[68] Iris Grossman, president of Women in Film, has similarly complimentary things to say about the Bullock sisters' production skill: "Sandra and Gesine illustrate that when two women set their minds on something, there is nothing they can't accomplish."[69]

Between 1998 and 2000, Fortis Films produced four more films: *Practical Magic*, which again saw Bullock pulling double duty as actress and producer; *Trespasses*; *Gun Shy* (with Bullock in a small role); and the wildly successful *Miss Congeniality*. This film grossed over $200 million at the box office and gave Fortis solid standing in Hollywood.

In addition to launching the ABC sit-com *George Lopez*, the first television series with an all-Latino cast, in 2002 Fortis Films produced *Two Weeks Notice* starring Bullock and Hugh Grant. This film presented an added challenge for Fortis, as it was the first movie to be filmed in New York City after the terrorist attacks on September 11, 2001. The attacks not only killed nearly three thousand people but destroyed the World Trade Center (also known as the Twin Towers) and surrounding blocks in Manhattan.

The iconic buildings were dramatically erased from the familiar New York skyline. Also temporarily destroyed was the economy of Lower Manhattan, as damaged businesses closed and tourists who had normally flocked to New York for its world-renowned restaurants, parks, shopping, and museums stayed away from the city that had suddenly become a terrorist target.

The significance of filming in a city that had changed so dramatically was not lost on Bullock, who witnessed the attacks firsthand from a hotel in downtown Manhattan. About her work on *Two Weeks Notice*, which was filmed over seventeen weeks in 2002, she says, "I think we had a really big responsibility, to show New York as the beautiful place that it is—with its brand new skyline. It was a New York that has never been shot."[70] The film did not dwell on the physical changes or New Yorkers' emotions in the months after the attacks. Instead, it accurately showed the

The popular film Miss Congeniality *starred Sandra Bullock (pictured with William Shatner) and also gave her production company Fortis Films a solid standing in Hollywood.*

Two Weeks Notice, *starring Sandra Bullock and Hugh Grant, was the first movie to be filmed in New York after the September 11, 2001 terrorist attacks.*

new New York City and proved to be another box office hit for Bullock and Fortis, grossing close to $200 million worldwide.

Celebrity Restaurateur

In 2002, Bullock expanded her business endeavors beyond the movie industry. Inspired by her mother's love of entertaining and her own appreciation of good food, she began work on what would become her first restaurant, Bess Bistro in Austin, Texas, where she had made her home for several years.

It was important to Bullock that customers not come to Bess Bistro simply to catch a glimpse of a famous movie star; she wanted them to have a great meal. To help the restaurant succeed on its own merits, Bullock hired executive chef Brenton Childs, who had experience in fine-dining restaurants elsewhere in Austin. Childs testifies that Bullock's restaurant was not the vanity project of a famous star. As he puts it, "She wanted to open a restaurant, and she happens to be a high-profile actress. But I imagine that if she wasn't a high profile actress she would

Because of her appreciation for good food, Bullock began the endeavor as restaurateur with the opening of Bess Bistro (pictured).

have built a restaurant anyhow. She just loves to eat and drink and have a good time with friends and family."[71]

After securing a chef, Bullock sought the perfect Austin location. She chose the Stratford Arms Building, a historic former bank. From start to finish, Bullock renovated, designed, and decorated the space according to her vision. Wanting to preserve the beauty of the existing structure, Bullock upgraded the space but kept many of the building's original features, such as exposed brick and wooden beams. It was not a quick project—the renovation and design process took more than four years—but ultimately Bullock ended up with a cozy yet elegant space for her restaurant.

Bullock also painstakingly created and fine-tuned the menu. Many of the dishes served at Bess Bistro originated at meetings with Bullock, her friends and family, and Childs. The group spent time remembering their favorite meals and family recipes, and enjoyed testing various dishes during evenings at home with friends. The final menu offered dishes that Bullock learned to love during her childhood in Europe, such as grilled quail and herb spaetzle, a kind of German dumpling.

In November 2006, Bullock opened Bess Bistro. Bullock chose the name Bess as "an homage to all the great madams who ran their establishments with the sole purpose of creating a retreat of great service, superb food and wine and an ambiance that allows the customers to let go and enjoy."[72] At first, some critics casually dismissed Bess Bistro as just another celebrity vanity project. As one early visitor to the restaurant said, "When movie stars open restaurants, do you really think the endeavor is about their love for food?"[73] The menu and the atmosphere that Bullock created at Bess Bistro soon won over even the most skeptical observers, though. In fact, *Austin Chronicle* reviewer Claudia Alarcon declared Bess Bistro her "new favorite place to go for a hearty meal, a glass of wine, and a fun time either alone or with friends."[74]

With the success of Bess Bistro, Bullock charged ahead with another restaurant venture in Austin called Walton's Fancy and Staple. Described on the store's website as a gourmet delicatessen/bakery and café, Walton's also offers event planning, floral, and

Bess Bistro Goes Green

When Bullock opened Bess Bistro in 2006, she wanted to ensure that the business was environmentally friendly. To this end, she and her staff put in place several practices and products that would minimize the restaurant's environmental impact. For example, instead of offering plastic forks and spoons for takeout orders, customers are given utensils made from biodegradable materials. The restaurant also shuns Styrofoam, and opts for packaging materials made from natural, renewable resources such as sugar cane. Bullock's commitment to environmentally friendly alternatives even applies to cleaning the grills at the restaurants. Instead of harsh chemicals that could pollute the environment, natural cleaning products such as vinegar, lemon juice, and baking soda are used.

catering services. Guests can order sandwiches and then shop for flowers and gifts while they wait for their food. The *Austin Chronicle* commented on the quality of Walton's Fancy and Staple upon its opening in 2009, describing it as "lovely and prosperous in a way rarely encountered in today's cost-cutting business environment."[75]

Soy Wonder

In addition to serving food and drinks, Bullock's restaurants are also sales outlets for yet another of her businesses: a soy candle company. Indeed, one of Bullock's favorite indulgences is taking a bath surrounded by lots of scented candles. When she looked into the candles she was using at home, however, Bullock was disappointed to realize that many products contained several harmful chemicals, including lead. In response, Bullock decided to start her own candle line called Bessence, a play on the name of her restaurant.

Sold online and in her Austin eateries, Bessence candles are made with soy, a natural and renewable resource, and special lead-free wicks. Her candles, which burn up to fifty hours, are handmade and environmentally friendly. "Everything, even the boxes, are recycled," she says. "Even the black spray that goes on the outside of [the box] is organic."[76] Available in four fragrances (Wild Bloomers, Black Cassis, Herbes avec Lagniappe, and Midnight Garden), the candles are made with plant- and flower-based essential oils. Bullock appeared on an Earth Day special of the *Oprah Winfrey Show* to talk about the candles, where she joked, "Yeah, [it's] something to fall back on [if acting doesn't work out]."[77]

Better to Give than to Receive

Bullock is not only interested in money-making pursuits, however. She has a charitable nature and has donated millions of dollars to a wide variety of causes and disaster relief efforts. After

Sandra Bullock has donated millions to charitable causes and disaster relief efforts. After Hurricane Katrina, Bullock provided Warren Easton Charter High School with new band uniforms and money for a scholarship program.

the September 11, 2001, terrorist attacks, for example, Bullock donated $1 million to the American Red Cross. Said Bullock, "This gift is to help the Red Cross provide care and comfort for the victims of tragedy and support for the families of the courageous men and women who give selflessly in the very worst of times, with hope that, someday, the terrible suffering of innocent people, such as the world so recently witnessed, will end."[78]

Bullock made a second $1 million donation to the Red Cross following the devastating tsunami that hit Asia in December 2004. Huge ocean waves caused by an underwater earthquake crashed onto the shores of Indonesia, Sri Lanka, and Thailand, killing more than 200,000 people and wiping out coastal areas. Following the disaster, massive relief was needed to help survivors rebuild their lives; some of that help came from the Red Cross using donations like Bullock's. About her donation, American Red Cross President Marsha J. Evans says, "Sandra continues to enable our lifesaving work and is a model for personal generosity."[79]

Bullock opened her wallet yet again when Hurricane Katrina struck New Orleans, Louisiana, on August 29, 2005, killing almost two thousand people and heavily damaging large parts of the city. The hurricane-force winds blew down trees and power lines, broke windows, and destroyed buildings throughout the city. The true catastrophe came when floodwaters broke through dozens of levees, the concrete walls that are supposed to protect the below-sea-level city from flooding. Some New Orleans neighborhoods were under fifteen feet (5m) of water, driving residents to wait for rescue on their rooftops.

Schools were among the many buildings destroyed in the Katrina disaster. Bullock helped by providing Warren Easton Charter High School with tens of thousands of dollars for a scholarship program, new band uniforms, and building renovations. Thanks in part to her efforts, the school reopened in 2006. Said Bullock when she attended the May 14, 2007, graduation of students, "You are the miracle that came out of this [disaster]."[80] In return for her generosity on behalf of the school, Bullock was inducted into the school's Hall of Fame.

When a massive 7.0 earthquake devastated the island nation of Haiti on January 12, 2010, Bullock stepped up once again. For the

During a benefit concert in Nashville, Tennessee, Sandra Bullock took the stage to help raise money for the victims of a devastating flood.

third time, she made a $1 million donation, this time to Médecins Sans Frontières (MSF), or Doctors Without Borders. This humanitarian group provides health care in poor or conflict-zone areas around the world. Bullock chose MSF because, she says, she "wanted to ensure that my donation would be used immediately to meet the needs of the Haitian people affected by this catastrophic event."[81] Her donation helped bring doctors to the area and helped establish temporary and more permanent health care centers around the island nation.

Bullock also took the stage in Nashville, Tennessee, to help raise money for victims of a disastrous flood that struck that city in May 2010. The sold-out event, called Nashville Rising: A Benefit Concert for Flood Recovery, aimed to raise $2 million in relief funds. The benefit was organized by country music stars Faith Hill and Tim McGraw, who played Bullock's husband in *The Blind Side*. Speaking at the benefit, Bullock acknowledged the strength of the citizens of Nashville: "They say a community is only as strong as its weakest link. And from where I stand, there are no weak links in this community."[82] She then picked up a guitar and played the opening notes of "Smoke on the Water" by Deep Purple. Bullock's was only a small part in the benefit, but it helped raise a significant amount of money for those affected.

"You Do It When You Can"

Bullock is quick to downplay her charitable contributions, saying, "Writing a check is easy when you've got it. The people who do the work ... are the ones that are amazing. ... [They] are the ones that really deserve the accolades."[83] Her reason for giving is honest and straightforward. "I was able to," she said of her help following the tsunami. "You do it when you can."[84] Although Bullock's fame comes from her starring roles in movies, her various business ventures and philanthropic efforts make clear that her interests are not limited to her acting career.

Chapter 5

Adding Wife and Stepmother to Her Résumé

A few years into the new millennium, Sandra Bullock had reached many professional milestones, but fewer personal ones. By the end of her thirties, she had not yet been married or had children, a fact that magazine articles increasingly drew attention to. Bullock resented this attention, and comparisons with other actresses her age, and was intent on drawing the line between her professional and personal life. As Bullock puts it, "There's a reason they call it private life."[85] Still, in the years to come, Bullock would make several important personal changes, including becoming a wife and stepmother, something she had never expected.

A Chance Meeting

For most of 2003, Bullock stayed out of the public eye. Other than a brief guest appearance on *George Lopez*, she was taking a break from acting. She kept herself busy working on her Austin restaurant, Bess Bistro, and enjoyed her free time with friends and family, especially around the holidays.

As Christmas approached, Bullock wanted to get something special for her eight-year-old godson. He told his famous godmother that he wanted to see a taping of *Monster Garage*, a cable

Sandra Bullock agreed to go on a date with Monster Garage *host Jesse James (pictured) after attending a taping of the show with her godson.*

TV show hosted by motorcycle builder Jesse James. *Monster Garage* featured teams of mechanics who took cars or jet skis and modified them into completely different, custom-made, working machines. For example, with a limited budget and in only seven days, a team would be tasked with changing a Mini Cooper into a snowmobile. The popular show was a favorite of Bullock's godson, but was new to Bullock. When she heard his request to attend a taping, she said, "I had no idea what he was talking about, but that's what he wanted so that's what he got."[86]

In addition to being unfamiliar with the show, Bullock was unfamiliar with the show's star and host, Jesse James. She remembers, "I had an image of an obese guy with a handlebar mustache."[87] When she and her godson arrived on set, she found a rugged, tattoo-covered man, someone she did not necessarily consider to be her type. As she tells it, "After that

Jesse James

Jesse Gregory James was born on April 19, 1969, in Lynwood, California. He began his career as a bodyguard, but his real interest was motorcycles. In 1992, he established West Coast Choppers, a custom motorcycle business based near Long Beach, California. His passion for motorcycles eventually translated into a reality television series called *Monster Garage* on the Discovery Channel.

In addition to his other work, James starred in the 2009 action/adventure reality series *Jesse James Is a Dead Man*. The show, which featured James attempting death-defying stunts, was an instant hit on Spike TV. Although she sometimes feared for his safety, Bullock could hardly complain about her husband's daredevil side. As she puts it, "I knew what I was getting into. Within three months of our relationship, he wrecked a car at 120 mph and almost died." Motorcycles and living dangerously are not James's only passion. In 2006, he opened an old-fashioned hamburger stand called Cisco Burger, named after one of his many beloved pet dogs.

Quoted in Stephen M. Silverman, "Sandra Bullock: My Husband Is Injury-Prone," *People*, March 5, 2007. www.people.com/people/article/0,,20014076,00.html.

meeting, Jesse tracked me down. I had no intention of going out with him."[88] Nevertheless, she put aside her preconceived notions of what a tattooed biker would be like, and agreed to go on a date.

A Private Romance

One date quickly turned into a new romance, one that Bullock was intent on hiding from the press. She had dated and broken up with several big-name stars in the past, including Tate Donovan and Ryan Gosling, and didn't feel it was positive or nurturing to go through love or heartache in the public eye. When

Jesse James and Sandra Bullock were intent on keeping their romance private and hidden from the press.

interviewed, she chose not to disclose information about her love life, even though magazine reporters had linked Bullock to James (the couple had been spotted together several times, including in a quiet café in Amsterdam). James, a television star himself, was not eager for the spotlight either.

When it came to their budding relationship, Bullock and James were protective not just with the public but also with each other. James had already been married twice before, and he wanted his relationship with Bullock to last. As James puts it, "I took my time and got to know her and did it right, and it was a great court-ship."[89] Bullock, who always thought of herself as very indepen-dent, became accustomed to letting James do things like open doors for her. She says, "It was so hard for me to allow someone to take care of me. ... But Jesse was like, Just let me do this."[90]

Although the couple was happily together for years, it didn't seem like marriage was part of their plans. Bullock was wary of marriage, even though her parents were married for almost 40 years. She was not interested in being someone's wife, and did not place the experience high on her life's to-do list. In part, Bullock was not interested in getting married because she did not want to find out afterward that she had married the wrong man. As she put it, "I would get so scared [whenever I thought about getting married] because my idea of marriage was not a very pleasant one."[91]

Blushing Bride

By 2005, however, Sandra's thoughts on marriage had changed, even though her love of privacy had not. That year, relatives and friends of the couple received invitations for an event to be held near Santa Barbara, California, on July 16. The invitations were for a barbecue to be thrown by James in honor of Bullock's upcoming forty-first birthday. The invitations did not mention anything about a wedding, but guests suspected that one might be close at hand. The couple did not live near Santa Barbara, and most guests would have to travel there from out of town to attend the barbecue. The invitation was also vague about the barbecue's exact location, which made guests suspect that the couple was trying to keep the festivities a secret. Finally, guests were asked to dress in cocktail attire, which seemed overly formal for a barbeque. As a result, many guessed, and hoped, that they would find themselves at a Bullock-James wedding, even though the couple had not announced an engagement.

On July 16, guests were shuttled from Santa Barbara north to the Folded Hills Ranch, located in the nearby city of Solvang. Fueling their suspicion that they had in fact been invited to a wedding, guests could not catch a glimpse of their host and hostess, who were nowhere to be found. Finally, around 7:30, as guests enjoyed cocktails under a party tent, they were shown a video of Bullock and James talking about their love and how much they meant to each other. At the end of the ten-minute video, James excitedly proclaimed, "We've been engaged since October, suckers!"[92]

After the video, bagpipers led guests from the tent to an open area surrounded by trees. Bullock wore cowboy boots and a white dress by designer Angel Sanchez. Her father, John, escorted her down a petal-strewn aisle to James, who waited for her under a large tree. A recording of Bullock's mother singing an aria was played. Younger sister Gesine also played an important part in the celebration. Not only was she the maid of honor, but she was also in charge of making the couple's four-tiered wedding cake (carrot with sour cream frosting) topped with a bride and groom on a bicycle. She also made a chocolate groom's cake that fed almost three hundred people. According to Gesine, "She was gorgeous. He was beautiful. They were very happy. It was nice for it all to finally happen."[93]

Loss Amid Joy

Although Bullock gained several family members in the 2000s, she also lost a very important one: her mother. In 1995, Bullock's mother Helga was diagnosed with colon cancer. Although as a young woman Bullock had had a strained relationship with her mother, in the face of illness, the dynamic between the two women changed completely. Bullock says, "We ceased to be mother and daughter. It was about a human being helping a human being."

For five years, the Bullock family rallied around Helga, spending time with her in the hospital, taking care of her while she was in hospice (a specialized care facility for terminally ill patients), and bringing her back to the family home in Arlington, Virginia, in her final days. In 2000, Helga Bullock passed away from colon cancer.

Quoted in Karen S. Schneider, "Calling Her Own Shots," *People,* April 4, 2005. www.people.com/people/archive/article/0,,20147269,00.html.

Sandra as Stepmom

When Bullock and James married, she became stepmother to James's three children: Chandler (10), Jesse Jr. (7), and Sunny (1). Chandler and Jesse Jr. lived with their mother near Bullock's and James's shared beachfront home in Long Beach, California. Bullock saw them often, but she was especially close to Sunny, who lived with the newlyweds. Both James and Bullock focused on providing a stable home for the children. Bullock took her role as stepmom seriously. Perhaps modeling herself after her own mother, she made sure that their homework was done and that the children were appropriately disciplined when they misbehaved. Bullock and James also frequently attended the children's various sports activities.

Not long after the couple married, rumors spread that Bullock was pregnant with the couple's biological child. The tabloids often issued conflicting reports on this subject, with one claiming Bullock was two months' pregnant and another saying she was four months' pregnant. Bullock and James insisted there was no truth to these rumors, which became increasingly annoying. Bullock thought of pregnancy as a private and sensitive issue. Fed up with the tabloid obsession over whether she was pregnant, she started saying, "Can I slap you now?"[94] to reporters who would not let the issue drop. The couple was finally forced to issue a statement on the matter, saying once and for all, "We are not with child, but we are pregnant with ideas."[95]

Bullock most resented questions about when she was going to have children because she viewed her stepchildren as her own children, even if she was not their biological mother. She said, "You don't have to give birth to someone to have a family. We're all family, an extended family."[96]

Taking Time Off to Be a Family

Contrary to early tabloid rumors of marital problems, Bullock and James were happy together. Bullock was James's biggest supporter when he appeared on the second season of *Celebrity Apprentice* (2009), a reality TV show in which celebrities compete to earn money for their favorite charity while working for business icon Donald Trump. Though James did not win, Bullock was proud of the way he presented himself as a hard-working and thoughtful person.

After her film *Premonition* was released in 2007, Bullock took two years off from acting to focus on her new family. She did not seem to miss show business. About this period in her life, Bullock said, "My greatest joy is making our home what it's supposed to be. Being a good wife, a good stepmom."[97] Before long, however, Bullock's priorities would drastically change, as she embarked on some of her most successful film roles and faced some of her most trying personal times.

Chapter 6

A Year of Triumphs and Challenges

When Bullock won both a Golden Globe and an Academy Award in 2010, she achieved not one but two goals that actresses in Hollywood aspire to. It was the pinnacle of her career. But personally, Bullock was about to face the biggest challenges of her life. During both troubles and celebrations, Bullock received an outpouring of support from friends and fans, and even gained the sympathies of Americans who had never particularly followed her career.

The Ultimate Betrayal

Just days after Bullock accepted her Academy Award on March 7, 2010, a tattoo model named Michelle McGee contacted reporters at *In Touch* magazine with an offer to sell the story that she had been Bullock's husband's mistress for several months. She claimed James cheated with her while Bullock was away filming *The Blind Side* in Atlanta, Georgia. Magazines, websites, and news networks locked onto the story. Bullock's fans were shocked by the news, as they had only heard great things from Bullock about her husband and her marriage. They were even more stunned when two other women came forward to acknowledge that James had also cheated with them. Like McGee, Melissa Smith met James online; Brigitte Daguerre met James when he hired her as a stylist for a photo shoot.

The Support of Her Fans and Friends

After news of the affairs broke, message boards and websites lit up with responses from concerned Bullock supporters. Comments posted on *People* magazine's site included such statements as, "Sandra, you are so much better and too classy for this drama!" and "Keep your head up and be strong. There are always bigger and better things out there."[98] Bullock's colleagues also rallied around the actress during her personal nightmare. For example,

George Lopez, a longtime friend of Sandra Bullock's, offered his support in the wake of Bullock's husband's infidelity.

Betty White, Bullock's costar in *The Proposal*, expressed support for the actress on the television show *Entertainment Tonight,* saying, "We're all deeply, deeply saddened. At such a high point in her life, it's tough, but I think the less other people have to say about it and let her work it out … the better."[99] George Lopez, a longtime friend of Bullock's, visited her often in the wake of James's infidelity. He said, "She knows how much I care about her. And, you know, when times are tough, friends step up."[100] Lopez stepped up for a friend who had supported him throughout his career and during his own personal difficulties, including a kidney transplant in 2005.

Indeed, people all over the country seemed to take the news of James's affairs personally. Fans and observers expressed sorrow that Bullock's Oscar celebration had been cut short—the actress had barely had time to bask in her success. The memory of Bullock's acceptance speeches for numerous awards in 2010, in which she lovingly acknowledged James and thanked him for always having her back, also fueled fans' sympathies. Bullock so publicly adored her husband and then was so publicly hurt by him that it was hard for the rest of the country not to feel hurt on her behalf.

In fact, James was so reviled by the public following the news of his numerous affairs that an article in *Entertainment Weekly* magazine referred to him as the "most hated man in America."[101] James was aware of his unpopularity; a friend said at one point that he was "sick of people thinking of him as a monster."[102] Yet the disgraced James knew he alone was responsible for the scandal and the strife it caused his family. As he said in a March 2010 statement, "There is only one person to blame for this whole situation, and that is me. It's because of my poor judgment that I deserve everything bad that is coming my way. This has caused my wife and kids pain and embarrassment beyond comprehension and I am extremely saddened to have brought this on them."[103]

Sensing how strongly the public supported Bullock, even the women who cheated with James expressed apologies to her. Michelle McGee went on the Australian show *Today Tonight* and said, "I'm sorry all this is public. I'm sorry for everything."[104]

Melissa Smith faxed Bullock a written apology, saying, "I am sorry for any hurt or pain that I have caused you. …I never meant you any harm."[105]

In an era when celebrities routinely discuss their personal troubles on Twitter or Facebook, or vent about their exes in tabloid magazines, Bullock remained silent about James's infidelity. She never spoke out against him and remained quiet amid the scandal. Her respectful handling of a devastating betrayal led the public to view her as a kind, classy person who deserved their sympathy. Bullock not only kept her opinions about the situation to herself, she also kept herself together. She did not react by stepping out with a brand-new boyfriend or by partying to escape her problems. Even people who had never before been Bullock's admirers appreciated how she handled the humiliating situation.

Going Into Hiding

Bullock was not merely quiet during the scandal; she went into hiding. When the scandal broke, Bullock was scheduled to appear at the premiere of *The Blind Side* in Berlin, Germany. She issued a simple statement that read, "Due to unforeseen personal reasons, a trip abroad to support *The Blind Side* has been deemed impossible at this time. I apologize for any inconvenience this may have caused and thank you for your continued support of the film."[106]

In the weeks that followed, Bullock gave no interviews, avoided having her picture taken, and disguised her whereabouts. Rumors swirled about where she was. Some gossip columnists speculated she was holed up at her home in Austin; others said she remained in Los Angeles. One publication reported that Bullock was with her sister in Vermont. Gesine was quick to shoot down that rumor, even providing receipts and airline tickets that proved she was in Chicago, Illinois, at the time. Gesine refused to disclose the whereabouts of her sister, saying, "[I am] deadly serious about my family, their privacy and even the most benign fictions printed about them."[107]

Not until April 19 did a photographer snap a picture of Bullock in public—this time without her wedding ring on. The image caused a stir in the media, which had not managed to get a clear photo of Bullock since her last public appearance, at the Academy Awards in March. Still, the media buzz generated by this photo was nothing compared to the buzz that followed Bullock's shocking revelation a few days later, announced on the cover of *People* magazine—a secret so carefully kept that only Bullock's closest friends and family knew about it.

Oh Boy! It's a Boy for Sandra Bullock!

In January 2010, Bullock and James had become adoptive parents of a baby boy named Louis Bardo Bullock, born on New Year's Day. Their adoption of Louis came through just before awards season.

Adoption in the United States

There are several kinds of adoption in the United States. One of the most common is adoption between people who are related in some way. An example of this is when a stepparent adopts a stepchild. Other adoptions take place between unrelated individuals, such as Bullock's adoption of Louis Bardo. The application process begins with a lot of paperwork to give as much possible information about the adoptive parents. In addition, a home study is completed. In this study, a professional observes behaviors and relationships of the adoptive parents in the home where the child will live. Adoption agencies do this to make sure that children are placed in safe, stable, and loving environments. Adoption can take up to several years and many thousands of dollars to complete. When successful, though it results in a loving home for a child in need.

Because Bullock was nominated for so many awards, she expected to be constantly in the spotlight. Not wanting to subject Louis to the impending media frenzy, she decided to keep the adoption a secret from the public.

Though Louis was placed with Bullock and James in 2010, the couple had actually begun the adoption process four years before. It took that long partly because the couple insisted on adopting an American-born child, and the adoption process in the United States is slower than in some foreign countries. Bullock and James had no preference for the child's gender or ethnic background. As James said, "My only prerequisite for adopting a baby: I want the baby that needs us the most."[108]

The couple also insisted that their celebrity status not afford them any shortcuts in the adoption process. Like any other prospective parents, Bullock and James had to fill out paperwork, undergo background checks, and open their home to inspection visits by the adoption agency. Said Bullock, "There are hoops, but the hoops are there to protect the child. And worth every jump."[109]

Louis was born in New Orleans, a city dear to Bullock, who feels strongly that he be raised there. Says Bullock, "New Orleans is his city, and he is going to know it inside and out."[110] Bullock and James purchased a five-bedroom house in the historic Garden District so that they could put down roots for their new son. In preparation for his New Orleans upbringing, they chose a house near the city's best schools.

Breaking the Big News

After more than a month of enduring the humiliating revelations of her husband's infidelity, Bullock was finally ready to share positive news with the world. The April 30, 2010, cover of *People* magazine featured a glowing Bullock and her adopted son with the headline "Meet My Baby!"[111] Fans and media outlets around the world were stunned; no one had known or even suspected that Bullock had adopted a baby. In retrospect, Bullock says there were several points at which her cover was nearly blown. For example,

The New Orleans Garden District

New Orleans, Louisiana, is a city full of history. Although it is perhaps best known for the lively bars and restaurants in the French Quarter, the Garden District of New Orleans is renowned for its stunning array of historic mansions. The Garden District was designed for houses with large gardens, but in the late 1800s, many of the formal gardens were divided and developed for additional homes. Today, these grand houses are admired by tourists and locals alike for their stately columns, unique wrought-iron fences, and massive trees surrounding the properties. Several of the houses have been declared National Historic Landmarks. Because this neighborhood is located above sea level, higher than other parts of the city, it was spared the terrible flooding that New Orleans suffered when Hurricane Katrina hit in 2005.

when she attended the Academy Awards, Bullock carried one of Louis's green socks in her bag. She kept dropping it on the ground and unsuspecting people kept handing it back to her, not realizing it was a clue to her new role as a mother. Another clue Bullock dropped that night came in her acceptance speech, when she said, "I would like to thank what this movie was about for me, which are the moms that take care of the babies and the children no matter where they come from."[112] Despite all the hints, Bullock's secret son remained sheltered from the media circus that surrounded his famous mother. Bullock herself admitted, "I don't know how we got away with it."[113]

Keeping this secret had become even more difficult once the news of James's affairs made headlines. Bullock recounts, "All I remember is thinking, 'I need to get Louis out of [the house]' before the vultures descend."[114] Bullock quickly moved out of the Southern California house she had shared with James and

Along with then-husband Jesse James, Sandra Bullock managed to keep the adoption of son Louis (pictured with Bullock) out of the spotlight.

avoided any kind of media exposure until she was ready to make her son's existence public.

When the adoption did become public knowledge, the news was well received. With her silence finally broken, Bullock was quick to gush about Louis: "He's just perfect, I can't even describe him any other way. It's like he's always been a part of our lives."[115]

At the same time Bullock publicly announced her adoption of Louis, she also filed for divorce from James after five years of marriage. On April 23, 2010, Bullock filed papers with a Texas court citing "discord or conflict of personalities that . . . prevents any reasonable expectations of reconciliation."[116] Until this announcement, fans and gossip columnists had speculated that Bullock and James might even reconcile, although she had moved out of their shared home. Reporters had a hard time finding the actual divorce filing: Bullock had kept it a secret by submitting the papers under the reverse of her initials, B.A.S., instead of her own name. With this news, however, it became official that Bullock was not going to stay married to James. About this decision, Bullock said only, "I'm sad, and I am scared."[117] The divorce was finalized just three months later. Divorce proceedings typically take several months, or even years. In this case, though, because neither Bullock nor James disagreed with the terms of the divorce, on June 28, 2010, Bullock's role as a wife was officially over and she was free to legally adopt Louis as a single mother. As for James, Bullock says, "I really don't know how our paths will intersect in the future, but the father I have known Jesse to be with all the kids is one that I hope Louis can experience one day, no matter how Jesse and I go on with our lives."[118]

Life Goes On

Once the media frenzy surrounding the affairs, the adoption, and her divorce calmed down, Bullock started to get on with her life, without self-pity. "[Brave is] the only thing that I ask myself to be," she once said. "Because no matter how many times I get knocked or I get blessed, it means that I'll always be able to go [on] again. And if I couldn't go [on], that would kill me."[119] Part of getting back to normal was returning to the public eye, and that spring offered her plenty of chances. In May 2010, MTV announced that Bullock would receive its Generation Award. According to MTV general manager Stephen Friedman, the award recognizes "her remarkable talent, amazing range of films and her visceral connection to our audience around the globe."[120] Bullock was the award's first female recipient.

The next month Bullock received the Troops Choice Award for Entertainer of the Year. In her acceptance speech, Bullock

In June 2010, Sandra Bullock—on stage with Bradley Cooper (left) and Scarlett Johansson (right)—accepted the MTV Generation Award.

acknowledged the difficult year she had endured in military terms, asking, "Did I win this for being entertainer of the year, or did I win this because of the spectacular I.E.D. [improvised explosive device] explosion that became my personal life?!"[121] The crowd responded with cheers and laughter, letting Bullock know she had their support. Said David Wild, *Rolling Stone* contributing editor and writer for the Guys Choice Awards, "In a year when so much news has been made all around her, Bullock returned to the public stage with great style and real heart."[122]

Bullock again took the opportunity to comment on her dizzying year at the MTV Movie Awards on June 6, 2010, when she accepted the MTV Generation Award. She joked about how expensive therapy is and how difficult it can be to take the high road—her way of acknowledging that she never said anything disparaging about James amid all the news of his scandalous affairs. She also took the opportunity to show that her divorce had not destroyed her, nor had her new identity as a mother forced her away from acting. "I love what I do," she said. "And I'm not going anywhere."[123]

Introduction: America's Sweetheart

1. Quoted in *Cosmopolitan*, "Sandra Bullock, on the Fast Lane to Stardom," November 1994.
2. Quoted in Jennet Conant, "America's Sweetheart," *Vanity Fair*, September 1995.
3. Anne Fletcher, "She's Strong, She's Sexy, She's Sandra Bullock," *Glamour*, June 2009. www.glamour.com/magazine/2009/06/ shes-strong-shes-sexy-shes-sandra-bullock?currentPage=2.
4. Barbara Schulgasser, "'In Love and War': A Farewell to Possibilities," *San Francisco Chronicle*, January 24, 1997. www.sfgate.com/cgi-bin/article.cgi?f=/e/a/1997/01/24/ WEEKEND11052.dtl.
5. sunflower777, "We love Sandra . . . , " Weblog comment, May 2, 2010, "Moving Vans Unload at Sandra Bullock's Gorgeous New Orleans Home," *Huffington Post*, April 29, 2010. www.huffingtonpost.com/2010/04/29/moving-vans- unload-at-san_n_557620.html.

Chapter 1: International Beginnings

6. Quoted in Chris Heath, "Sweet dreams are made of this," *Premiere* (UK), September 1995.
7. Sandra Bullock, interview by Tavis Smiley, *Tavis Smiley: Late Night on PBS*, KCET-PBS, January 12, 2010. www.pbs .org/kcet/tavissmiley/archive/201001/20100112_bullock .html.
8. Quoted in Holly Millea, "The Secret Life of Sandra Bullock," *Premiere* (USA), April 2000.
9. Quoted in Michael Callahan, "Sandra Bullock Plays Survivor, *Marie Claire,* May 2002, pp. 80–82.
10. Quoted in Millea, "The Secret Life of Sandra Bullock."
11. Quoted in Millea, "The Secret Life of Sandra Bullock."
12. Bullock, interview by Tavis Smiley.
13. Quoted in Heath, "Sweet dreams are made of this."

14. Quoted in Heath, "Sweet dreams are made of this."
15. Quoted in Kristin O'Neill, "Girl on Top," *Premiere* (USA), July 1996.
16. Quoted in Fletcher, "She's Strong, She's Sexy, She's Sandra Bullock."
17. Quoted in *Vogue* (UK), "Sandra Bullock: Box Office Goddess," October 1996.
18. Quoted in Callahan, "Sandra Bullock Plays Survivor."
19. Quoted in Jeanne Wolf, "Sandra Bullock: 'I'm Aware That I Can Be Annoying,'" *Parade*, October 29, 2009. www.parade .com/celebrity/celebrity-parade/2009/1029-sandra-bullock .html.
20. Quoted in Liza Hamm, "Sandra Bullock: Mom Was the Life of the Party," *People*, September 30, 2009. www.people.com/ people/article/0,,20309116,00.html.
21. Quoted in Oprah.com, "How Sandra Bullock Lives Green," January 1, 2006. www.oprah.com/world/Tour-Sandra-Bullocks-Eco-Friendly-Austin-Eatery/1.
22. Quoted in *People,* "Sandra Bullock: Actress," May 10, 1999. www.people.com/people/archive/article/0,,20128191,00 .html.
23. Quoted in *Vogue* (UK), "Sandra Bullock: Box Office Goddess."
24. Quoted in Linda Das, "Sandra's Biggest Hitch," *Mail Online*, July 14, 2009. www.mailonsunday.co.uk/home/you/article-1198116/Sandras-biggest-hitch.html.
25. Quoted in *InStyle*, "You Asked, Sandra Answered," March 2009. www.instyle.com/instyle/package/general/photos/ 0,,20310478_20257367_20575595,00.html.
26. Quoted in *Vogue* (UK), "Sandra Bullock: Box Office Goddess."
27. Quoted in Heath, "Sweet dreams are made of this."
28. Quoted in Mihaela Stroia, "Sandra Bullock's Nightmares," October 7, 2005. www.irishexaminer.com/breakingnews/ ireland/cwcweymhauid/.
29. Quoted in *Cosmopolitan*, "Sandra Bullock, on the Fast Lane to Stardom."
30. Quoted in Heath, "Sweet dreams are made of this."

31. Mel Gussow, "Review/Theater; Ketron's 'No Time Flat,'" *New York Times*, May 5, 1988. www.nytimes.com/1988/05/05/theater/review-theater-ketron-s-no-time-flat.html.
32. Quoted in Heath, "Sweet dreams are made of this."

Chapter 2: Speeding to Success

33. Quoted in Conant, "America's Sweetheart."
34. Eugene Levy, "Love Potion No. 9," *Variety*, November 13, 1992. www.variety.com/review/VE1117900059.html.
35. Quoted in Heath, "Sweet dreams are made of this."
36. Quoted in Heath, "Sweet dreams are made of this."
37. Hal Hinson, "'Demolition Man,'" *Washington Post*, October 9, 1993. www.washingtonpost.com/wp-srv/style/longterm/movies/videos/demolitionmanrhinson_b007c3.htm.
38. Quoted in Alexis Chiu, "Sandra Bullock & Keanu Reeves," *People*, June 26, 2006. www.people.com/people/archive/article/0,,20061287,00.html.
39. Quoted in Chiu, "Sandra Bullock & Keanu Reeves."
40. Quoted in Fred Schruers, "Speed Freak," *Rolling Stone*, June 26, 1997.
41. Quoted in *Cosmopolitan*, "Sandra Bullock, on the Fast Lane to Stardom."
42. Quoted in Heath, "Sweet dreams are made of this."
43. James Berardinelli, "Speed," Reelviews.net, June 1994. www.reelviews.net/php_review_template.php?identifier=141.
44. Quoted in Heath, "Sweet dreams are made of this."
45. Quoted in Gregory Cerio, "Speeding Bullock," *People*, August 14, 1995. www.people.com/people/archive/article/0,,20101321,00.html
46. Quoted in Roald Rynning, "A Load of Bullock," *Film Review* (UK), October 1995.
47. Roger Ebert, "While You Were Sleeping," *Chicago Sun-Times*, April 21, 1995. http://rogerebert.suntimes.com/apps/pbcs.dll/article?AID=/19950421/REVIEWS/504210307/1023.
48. Quoted in *Vogue* (UK), "Sandra Bullock: Box Office Goddess."
49. Quoted in Demetrios Matheou, "Upfront, Down-to-Earth," *Telegraph*, June 18, 2002. www.telegraph.co.uk/culture/film/3578999/Upfront-down-to-earth.html.

50. Desson Howe, "'Speed 2': That Sinking Feeling," *Washington Post*, June 13, 1997. www.washingtonpost.com/wp-srv/style/longterm/movies/review97/speed2howe.htm.

51. Stephen Hunter, "'Speed': Missing a Hook and Line, It's a Stinker," *Washington Post*, June 13, 1997. www.washingtonpost.com/wp-srv/style/longterm/movies/review97/speed2hunter.htm.

Chapter 3: Making Movies, Making History

52. Quoted in BBC News, "Bullock Honoured on Walk of Fame," March 25, 2005. http://news.bbc.co.uk/2/hi/entertainment/4382239.stm.

53. Quoted in Mark Dagostino and Chris Gardner, "Insider," *People*, April 11, 2005. www.people.com/people/archive/article/0,,20147316,00.html.

54. Geoff Berkshire, "'The Proposal' Review," *Metromix*, June 18, 2009. http://chicago.metromix.com/movies/movie_review/the-proposal-review/1255571/content.

55. Quoted in John Harlow, "Sandra Bullock on having her moment," *Sunday Times Online* (London), March 14, 2010. http://entertainment.timesonline.co.uk/tol/arts_and_entertainment/film/article7055135.ece?loc=interstitialskip.

56. Mick LaSalle, "The Blind Side," *San Francisco Chronicle*, November 20, 2009. www.sfgate.com/cgi-bin/article.cgi?f=/c/a/2009/11/20/MVBI1ALUN6.DTL.

57. Quoted in Pamela McClintock, "Sandra Bullock Makes History," *Variety*, January 4, 2010. www.variety.com/article/VR1118013301.html?categoryid=1236&cs=1.

58. Peter Travers, "The Proposal," *Rolling Stone*, June 18, 2009. www.rollingstone.com/movies/reviews/8550/51246.

59. Betsy Sharkey, "'Review: The Blind Side'," *Los Angeles Times*, November 20, 2009. http://articles.latimes.com/2009/nov/20/entertainment/la-et-blind-side20-2009nov20.

60. Claudia Puig, "Strong Acting Can't Outrun Shallow Tale in 'The Blind Side,'" *USA Today*, November 20, 2009. www.usatoday.com/life/movies/reviews/2009-11-20-blindside20_ST_N.htm.

61. Quoted in Catherine Donaldson-Evans et al., "Sandra Bullock 'Stunned' by Two Golden Globe Nominations,"

People, December 15, 2010. www.people.com/people/article/ 0,,20327382,00.html.

62. Quoted in Access Hollywood, "2010 Golden Globes: Backstage with Sandra Bullock," January 17, 2010. www .accesshollywood.com/2010-golden-globes-backstage-with-sandra-bullock_video_1195762.

63. Quoted in Scott Huver, "Sandra Bullock: 'I'm *So* Not Winning an Oscar,'" *People*, February 6, 2010. www .peoplestylewatch.com/people/stylewatch/package/article/ 0,,20332759_20342270,00.html.

64. Sandra Bullock, Academy Award acceptance speech, March 7, 2010. http://oscar.go.com/video/index?playlist Id=253172&clipId=253249.

Chapter 4: Offscreen Successes

65. Quoted in Minju Pak, "All in the Family," *Hollywood Reporter*, June 10, 2005. www.hollywoodreporter.com/hr/search/article_ display.jsp?vnu_content_id=1000954623.

66. Quoted in Pak, "All in the Family."

67. Quoted in Zoe Heller, "Two for the Road," *Harper's Bazaar*, April 1999.

68. Quoted in Jonathan Van Meter, "The Producer," *Vogue*, March 2005.

69. Quoted in Pak, "All in the Family."

70. Quoted in Matheou, "Upfront, Down-to-Earth."

71. Quoted in Alexis Chiu, "Sandra Bullock: 'I Have My Family,'" *People*, March 26, 2007. www.people.com/people/archive/ article/0,,20061646,00.html.

72. Quoted in Laura Kelso, "Bess Bistro on Pecan," *Austin Monthly*, March 2007, p. 162. www.bessbistro.com/images/ austin_monthly_0307.pdf.

73. Kelso, "Bess Bistro on Pecan," p. 162.

74. Claudia Alarcon, "Bess Bistro on Pecan," *Austin Chronicle*, February 9, 2007. www.austinchronicle.com/gyrobase/ Issue/review?oid=oid:444384.

75. Kate Thornberry, "Restaurant Reviews: Walton's Fancy and Staple," *Austin Chronicle*, July 17, 2009. www.austinchronicle .com/gyrobase/Issue/review?oid=oid%3A810659.

76. Quoted in Oprah.com, "How Sandra Bullock Lives Green."
77. Quoted in Brian Orloff, "Sandra Bullock Helps Save the Earth—with Candles," *People*, April 22, 2008. www.people .com/people/article/0,,20193972,00.html.
78. Quoted in American Red Cross press release, September 24, 2001. http://216.203.22.52/page.php/prmID/232.
79. Quoted in Associated Press, "Bullock Donates $1 Million to Tsunami Relief," January 3, 2005. http://today.msnbc.msn .com/id/6781783/38692349.
80. Quoted in Alicia Dennis, "Sandra Bullock Honors New Orleans Graduates," *People*, May 15, 2007. www.people .com/people/article/0,,20038963,00.html.
81. Quoted in Nicole Eggenberger, "Sandra Bullock Donates $1 Million to Doctors Without Borders," *OK*, January 15, 2010. www.okmagazine.com/2010/01/sandra-bullock-donates-1-million-to-doctors-without-borders/.
82. Quoted in Cindy Watts, "Sandra Bullock Blindsides Audience with Nashville Rising Appearance," *Tennessean*, June 23, 2010. http://blogs.tennessean.com/tunein/2010/06/23/sandra-bullock-blindsides-audience-with-nashville-rising-appearance/.
83. Quoted in ETOnline.com, "Sandra Bullock's Post-Katrina Hall of Fame Honor," May 18, 2009. www.etonline.com/news/2009/05/74292/.
84. Quoted in Karen S. Schneider, "Calling Her Own Shots," *People*, April 4, 2005. www.people.com/people/archive/article/0,,20147269,00.html.

Chapter 5: Adding Wife and Stepmother to Her Résumé

85. Quoted in Schneider, "Calling Her Own Shots."
86. Quoted in Louis B. Hobson, "Q&A with Sandra Bullock," *Calgary Sun*, June 11, 2006. http://jam.canoe.ca/Movies/2006/06/11/1625512.html.
87. Quoted in Fletcher, "She's Strong, She's Sexy, She's Sandra Bullock."
88. Quoted in Wolf, "Sandra Bullock."

89. Quoted in Michelle Tauber, "So in Love," *People*, July 31, 2006. www.people.com/people/archive/article/0,,20157723,00. html.

90. Quoted in Christine Lennon, "Sandra Bullock: Myth & Reality," *Harper's Bazaar*, June 2009. www.harpersbazaar .com/magazine/cover/sandra-bullock-0609.

91. Quoted in Van Meter, "The Producer."

92. Quoted in Karen S. Schneider, "Surprise Party," *People*, August 1, 2005. www.people.com/people/archive/article/ 0,,20143948,00.html.

93. Quoted in Schneider, "Surprise Party."

94. Quoted in Stephen M. Silverman, "Sandra Bullock: Stop Asking When I'll Have Kids," *People*, February 13, 2007. www.people.com/people/article/0,,20011651,00.html.

95. Quoted in "Sandra Bullock & Jesse James: We're Not Expecting," *People*, November 20, 2006. www.people.com/ people/article/0,,1564878,00.html.

96. Quoted in Lennon, "Sandra Bullock."

97. Quoted in Brian Orloff, "Sandra Bullock Calls Being a Wife & Stepmom Her Greatest Joy," *People*, February 10, 2009. www.people.com/people/article/0,,20257966,00 .html.

Chapter 6: A Year of Triumphs and Challenges

98. Marcia Ophelia and Leanna Piane, Weblog comments, "Sandra Bullock Pulls Out of London Premiere," *People*, March 17, 2010. www.people.com/people/article/0,,20352311,00 .html.

99. Quoted in Tim Nudd, "Betty White 'Deeply Saddened' for Sandra Bullock," *People*, March 23, 2010. www.people.com/ people/article/0,,20353909,00.html.

100. Quoted in *People*, "George Lopez Happy to 'Step Up' for Sandra Bullock," April 16, 2010. www.people.com/people/ article/0,,20361521,00.html.

101. Dan Snierson, "Jesse James: Most Hated Man in America," *Entertainment Weekly*, April 2, 2010. www.ew.com/ew/article/ 0,,20358860,00.html.

102. Quoted in *People,* "Source: Jesse James 'Sick of People Thinking He's a Monster,'" May 28, 2010. www.people .com/people/article/0,,20388559,00.html.

103. Quoted in Elizabeth Leonard, "Jesse James Apologizes to Sandra Bullock and His Children," *People*, March 19, 2010. www.people.com/people/article/0,,20352642,00.html.

104. Quoted in Brian Orloff, "Michelle McGee Apologizes to Sandra Bullock," *People*, April 12, 2010. www.people.com/people/article/0,,20360264,00.html.

105. Quoted in "Jesse's Mistress to Sandra: So Sorry," TMZ.com, April 26, 2010. http://tmz.vo.llnwd.net/o28/newsdesk/tmz_documents/0425_MelissaSmith_SandraBullock.pdf.

106. Quoted in *People,* "Sandra Bullock Pulls Out of London Premiere," March 17, 2010. www.people.com/people/article/0,,20352311,00.html.

107. Quoted in Steven M. Silverman, "Bullock's Sister Sets Record Straight on Sandra's Whereabouts," *People*, April 18, 2010. www.people.com/people/article/0,,20361914,00.html.

108. Quoted in Tim Nudd, "Jesse James Says Baby Louis Brought Him and Sandra Bullock Closer," *People*, May 25, 2010. www.people.com/people/package/article/0,,20364464_20388202,00.html.

109. Quoted in J.D. Heylman and Alexis Chiu, "Loving Louis," *People*, May 10, 2010, p. 172.

110. Quoted in Kristin Boehm, "Sandra Bullock's Ties to New Orleans," *People*, April 28, 2010. www.people.com/people/package/article/0,,20364464_20364811,00.html.

111. Quoted in *People,* "World Exclusive: Meet Sandra Bullock's Baby Boy!" April 28, 2010. www.people.com/people/article/0,,20364639,00.html.

112. Bullock, Academy Award acceptance speech.

113. Quoted in Heylman and Chiu, "Loving Louis," p. 171.

114. Quoted in Heylman and Chiu, "Loving Louis," p. 178.

115. Quoted in *People,* "World Exclusive."

116. Quoted in Access Hollywood, "Sandra Bullock & Jesse James Finalize Divorce," June 28, 2010. www.accesshollywood.com/movies/sandra-bullock-and-jesse-james-finalize-divorce_article_33949.

117. Quoted in Heylman and Chiu, "Loving Louis," p. 180.
118. Quoted in Heylman and Chiu, "Loving Louis," p.180.
119. Quoted in Schruers, "Speed Freak."
120. Quoted in Eric Ditzian, "Sandra Bullock to Receive Generation Award at MTV Movie Awards," MTV.com, May 26, 2010. www.mtv.com/news/articles/1640110/20100526/story .jhtml.
121. Quoted in Reagan Alexander and Scott Huver, "Sandra Bullock Makes Surprise Appearance for the 'Guys,'" *People*, June 6, 2010. www.people.com/people/article/0,,20391618,00.html.
122. David Wild, "'Sophisticated Lady': One Guy's Playlist for the Classy Return of Sandra Bullock," *Huffington Post*, June 6, 2010. www.huffingtonpost.com/david-wild/sophisticated-lady-one-gu_b_602101.html.
123. Quoted in Stephen M. Silverman, "Sandra Bullock Is 'Not Going Anywhere,'" *People*, June 6, 2010. www.people.com/people/article/0,,20391658,00.html.

1964

Sandra Annette Bullock is born in Arlington, Virginia, on July 26 to John and Helga Bullock.

1970

Bullock's sister and longtime business partner Gesine is born.

1974

John Bullock is severely injured in a bulldozer accident.

1982

Bullock graduates from Washington-Lee High School in Arlington, Virginia.

1986

Bullock leaves East Carolina University in Greenville, North Carolina, just short of a degree, to move to New York City.

1990

Bullock is cast in the short-lived TV series *Working Girl*; appears in *Fire on the Amazon*.

1992

Love Potion No. 9 is released.

1993

Bullock costars with Sylvester Stallone and Wesley Snipes in *Demolition Man*.

1994

Speed grosses almost $15 million on its opening weekend and catapults Bullock into the public eye.

1995

While You Were Sleeping earns Bullock her first Golden Globe nomination; thriller *The Net* takes in $50 million at the box office. Both films assure her bankability as an actress.

1996

Bullock establishes her own production company, Fortis Films.

1997

Bullock reprises her role as Annie Porter in the sequel *Speed 2: Cruise Control*. *Making Sandwiches*, a short film she wrote, acted in, directed, and produced, is screened at the Sundance Film Festival.

2000

Bullock earns her second Golden Globe nomination for her work in *Miss Congeniality*.

2000–2002

After losing her mother, Helga, to cancer in 2000, Bullock takes a break from acting.

2003

Bullock meets Jesse James for the first time after arranging for her godson to meet the popular motorcycle builder.

2004

The ensemble cast of *Crash*, which includes Bullock, earns a Screen Actors Guild Award for Outstanding Performance by a Cast in a Motion Picture.

2005

Bullock marries longtime boyfriend Jesse James on July 16 at a surprise wedding ceremony in Solvang, California.

2006

Bess Bistro, Bullock's restaurant in Austin, Texas, opens for business.

2009

Bullock stars in three movies: *The Proposal*, *All About Steve*, and *The Blind Side*. Although *All About Steve* is not a box-office hit, *The Proposal* and *The Blind Side* gross more than $150 million and $250 million in theaters, respectively.

December 2009–March 2010

Bullock receives two Golden Globe nominations, two Razzie nominations, and an Oscar nomination for her work in *The Proposal*, *All About Steve*, and *The Blind Side*. She wins a Golden Globe for Best Actress in a Motion Picture–Drama, Razzies for Worst Actress and Worst Couple, and the Academy Award for Best Actress. Days after winning her Oscar, news breaks of her husband's infidelity.

April 2010

In *People* magazine, Bullock goes public with the news of her adopted son Louis Bardo. She also announces that she has filed for divorce from James.

July 23, 2010

Bullock and James are legally divorced.

August 2010

Forbes magazine names Bullock the highest-paid actress in Hollywood.

For More Information

Books

Gesine Bullock-Prado, *My Life from Scratch: A Sweet Journey of Starting Over, One Cake at a Time.* New York: Broadway, 2009. Written by Bullock's sister Gesine, this book features stories and recipes from the author's life.

Michael Lewis, *The Blind Side* (Movie Tie-in Edition). New York: W. W. Norton, 2009. This book, which is the basis of Bullock's 2009 film, details the real-life story of the Tuohy family and their adoption of Michael Oher.

Periodicals

Elaine Aradillas, "Inside George Lopez and Sandra Bullock's Friendship," *People*, April 10, 2010. www.people.com/people/article/0,,20359564,00.html.

Earl Dittman, "Interview: Ryan Reynolds and Sandra Bullock, *The Proposal*," *Driven*, October 14, 2010. www.drivenmag.com/2009/10/14/interview-ryan-reynolds-and-sandra-bullock-onthe-proposal/.

Anne Fletcher, "She's Strong, She's Sexy, She's Sandra Bullock," *Glamour*, June 2009.

Louis B. Hobson, "Q&A with Sandra Bullock," *Calgary Sun*, June 11, 2006. http://jam.canoe.ca/Movies/2006/06/11/1625512.html.

Christine Lennon, "Sandra Bullock: Myth & Reality," *Harper's Bazaar*, June 2009.

Demetrios Matheou, "Upfront, Down-to-Earth," *Telegraph*, June 18, 2002. www.telegraph.co.uk/culture/film/3578999/Upfront-down-to-earth.html.

Karen S. Schneider, "Calling Her Own Shots," *People*, April 4, 2005. www.people.com/people/archive/article/0,,20147269,00.html.

Jeanne Wolf, "Sandra Bullock: 'I'm Aware That I Can Be Annoying,'" *Parade*, October 29, 2009.

Internet Sources

Access Hollywood, "Sandra Bullock & Jesse James Finalize Divorce," June 28, 2010. www.accesshollywood.com/movies/sandra-bullock-and-jesse-james-finalize-divorce_article_33949.

Sandra Bullock, Academy Award acceptance speech, March 7, 2010. http://oscar.go.com/video/index?playlistId=253172&clipId=253249.

Sandra Bullock, Golden Globe interview, January 17, 2010. http://www.goldenglobes.org/videogallery/video/49942/

Sandra Bullock, interview by Tavis Smiley, *Tavis Smiley: Late Night on PBS*, KCET-PBS, January 12, 2010. www.pbs.org/kcet/tavissmiley/archive/201001/20100112_bullock.html.

The Insider, "Sandra Bullock: Biography." http://www.theinsider.com/celebrities/Sandra_Bullock

Websites

The Blind Side (www.theblindsidemovie.com) The official website of the movie offers videos, photos, downloads, and almost a dozen pages of production notes related to this award-winning film.

Fandango's Sandra Bullock Filmography (www.fandango.com/sandrabullock/filmography/p9472) This movie-themed site includes a complete list of all of Bullock's films, which users can sort by title or release date.

The Proposal (www.myspace.com/proposalmovie) Visitors to this official Myspace page can access free downloads such as wallpaper and buddy icons, watch clips from the movie, and check out a photo gallery of the film's stars.

Cover Photo: John Shearer/Getty Images Entertainment/Getty Images

20th Century Fox Television/The Kobal Collection/The Picture Desk, 24

20th Century Fox/The Kobal Collection/Foreman, Richard/The Picture Desk, 29

20th Century Fox/The Kobal Collection/Loss, Christine/The Picture Desk, 48

AP Images, 22

AP Images/Jean-Marc Bouju, 60

AP Images/Dan Steinberg, 43

AP Images/Matt Sayles, 45, 76

AP Images/Mark J. Terrill, 62

Cary Darling/MCT/Landov, 52

Castle Rock/Fortis/The Kobal Collection/Batzdorff, Ron/The Picture Desk, 49

Fred Breedon/Nashville Rising/Getty Images, 57

James Crump/Getty Images, 55

Jon Furniss/WireImage/Getty Images, 40

Jon Kopaloff/FilmMagic/Getty Images, 9

Karin Cooper/Getty Images, 18

Kevin Winter/Getty Images, 34

Lester Cohen/WireImage/Getty Images, 31

Marcel Thomas/FilmMagic/Getty Images, 74

Seth Poppel Yearbook Library, 19, 21

SGranitz/WireImage/Getty Images, 38

Steve Granitz/WireImage/Getty Images, 68

Todd Williamson/FilmMagic/Getty Images, 14

Warner Bros Pictures/The Kobal Collection/The Picture Desk, 42

Warner Bros/Silver Pictures/The Kobal Collection/The Picture Desk, 28

Warner Bros/The Kobal Collection/Reed, Eli/The Picture Desk, 50

Warner Bros/The Kobal Collection/The Picture Desk, 10

Sandy Gade Algra earned her bachelor's degree in Italian studies from New York University in 1999. She has worked as a writer and editor since 2000. Algra lives with her husband, Jeffrey, in Brooklyn, New York, but visits friends and family in San Diego, California, and Amsterdam, the Netherlands, whenever she can.